THE PARENT & CHILD SERIES

PREGNANCY AND YOUR BABY'S FIRST YEAR

Also by Lawrence Kutner, Ph.D.

Parent & Child: Getting Through to Each Other

THE PARENT & CHILD SERIES

PREGNANCY
AND YOUR BABY'S
FIRST YEAR

Lawrence Kutner, Ph.D.

WILLIAM MORROW AND COMPANY, INC.
New York

Library of Congress Cataloging in Publication Data

Kutner, Lawrence.
    Pregnancy and Your Baby's First Year / Lawrence Kutner.
       p.   cm.
    ISBN 0-688-10215-8
    1. Infants. 2. Infants—Development. 3. Infants—Care.
4. Parenting. 5. Infants—United States. I. Title.
HQ774.K58 1993
305.23'2—dc20   92-20808
                                                                               CIP

Printed in the United States of America

2 3 4 5 6 7 8 9 10

BOOK DESIGN BY DEBBY JAY

ACKNOWLEDGMENTS

Never try to move your home and write a book at the same time. The two are completely incompatible. Each by itself will strain your personal and professional relationships. Together, they make a writer insufferable to be around. And so, I begin this book with a few words of thanks to the people who stuck with me when I was crabby and intolerant, as well as those who have helped me with my books and my *New York Times* and *Parents Magazine* columns.

Adrian Zackheim and Mark Gompertz, my editors at William Morrow and Company and Avon Books, respectively, have been patient beyond belief as my manuscript slowly turned into a book. In addition to their editorial acumen, their experiences as fathers helped me focus my writing on what's really useful to parents.

Al Lowman, my literary agent, has helped me put more of myself into my writing—including the sometimes-strange sense of humor we share.

Joanne Reilly Lamb, my assistant and general factotum when I lived in Minneapolis, not only organized my life, but gave me tremendous insight into the plight of working parents. Together we created what has been called a cross between a newsroom and a child-care center—which may be a redundant description.

Stephen Drucker, Yanick Rice Lamb, Penelope Green, and Mary Curtis, my editors at *The New York Times*, have guided my writing and encouraged me to look at important issues that other parenting columnists have ignored.

Amy Genova, my editor at *Parents Magazine*, has been a delight to work with. Her understanding of what parents want to know has helped me focus my work.

Barry Garfinkel, M.D., the chief of child and adolescent psychiatry at the University of Minnesota and a good friend, taught me a lot about how children's minds work.

T. Berry Brazelton, M.D., an incredible man who has changed how we all look at and treat children, welcomed me as a colleague and shared his insights on child development and parent-child communication.

Michael Jellinek, M.D., the chief of child psychiatry at Massachusetts General Hospital, recruited me to teach at Harvard Medical School, helped with my family's transition to life in Cambridge, and provided guidance on several of the topics in this book.

Doug Fizel, of the American Psychological Association, has helped me for several years track down sources of up-to-date information about child development and parent-child communication.

Anne Petersen, Ph.D., formerly the dean of the College of Health and Human Development at Pennsylvania State University, and now the dean of the Graduate School at the University of Minnesota, has provided tremendous support through her recognition of the need to translate scientific and academic information about child development into language that parents can understand and use.

The hundreds of psychologists, psychiatrists, and other professionals from around the United States and Canada who've taken the time to share with me their insights and research findings, have formed the underpinnings of this book. Without their contributions, my job would be impossible.

Cheryl Olson, my wife, has been immensely supportive, even while enduring the stress of finishing her doctorate in public health. I feel tremendously lucky just to know her, let alone be married to her.

Finally, our son Michael has shown me what all these theories of child development that I've studied and taught are really about. This book, which was written during his second and third years of life, has given him the opportunity to provide me with constant feedback. His most telling comment came just after his second birthday. I had been writing furiously for several weeks and, I must admit, not paying as much attention to him as either of us might have wanted. One evening, when he was playing with his toy trucks, I asked him if he wanted to cuddle up and read a book with me. He looked up and said, "Not now, Daddy. I'm working!"

Through those simple words he told me that I had to cut back on my writing schedule. I did. After all, I know what's really important.

CONTENTS

INTRODUCTION

It was four-thirty in the morning—an hour which, until a few weeks earlier, would have found my eyes tightly shut with sleep. But that morning my two-month-old son acted as if he were trying to break some sort of record. I'd fed him his bottle before putting him to bed. My wife had changed him at one A.M. when his cries announced a wet diaper. When he loudly complained of hunger at four o'clock, it was my turn to take care of him.

The problem wasn't the feeding, which I enjoyed, but its aftermath. Like many babies, he usually spat up a bit of formula after finishing a bottle. This morning his stomach was bothering him and he was spewing forth partially digested formula with a vengeance. Every time I'd clean him, he'd spit up again, dirtying his clothes and, more often than not, mine as well.

As he did this for the sixth time (he had just broken his previous record) I found myself having an unexpected thought: *He's doing this out of spite!*

All of my psychology training and all of the words I'd written about child development abandoned my sleep-deprived brain and were replaced by the heartfelt belief that my two-month-old son was consciously and maliciously out to get me.

The pattern had become clear over the past few minutes. He couldn't just spit up twice on the same garment. No, he would shrewdly wait until I had changed him so that he could wreak his particular havoc as effectively as possible. His piercing cries and thrashing limbs made getting him into clean clothes more difficult for both of us, of course. It was all part of his plan, I thought. We had become like cat and mouse, each waiting for the other to make a move.

Soon I found myself anticipating the results of his gastric distress as if it were a perverse game. Which of us could outlast the other? Would my supply of clothes outstretch his reservoir of food? Over the next few minutes he spat up twice more—acts I interpreted as confirmation of his dastardly scheme against me. Our battle was engaged, and I told myself that I would be the victor.

Just then my wife walked into the nursery. She had been unable to sleep through the combination of his crying and my muffled curses. I told her that he had been through *eight* changes of clothes in the past half hour. She looked at me incredulously. "Why don't you just put a bib on him?" she asked.

I begin this book with that story to dissuade you of any illusion you might have that I know all the answers when it comes to child development. Every time I think, rather grandiosely, that I completely understand some aspect of childhood, my son or some other child comes up with an effective way of letting me know I'm not so smart.

I've noticed that many books aimed at parents purport to have "the answer" to raising children successfully—an approach rooted more firmly in marketing than in science. It also fosters guilt among parents. Since the authors claim their advice will work for every child, if it fails, that must mean that you, the parent, are doing something wrong. This is nonsense—and it's also the last thing a parent who's under stress needs to hear.

Some concepts (such as the natural history of childhood— what behaviors are normal and to be expected at different

stages of development) and techniques (like behavior modi-
fication, time out, and allowing children to see the natural
consequences of their actions) are tremendously powerful
tools for parents. But using those tools requires both flexibility
and insight. You can't simply charge ahead with an approach
that doesn't take your specific children or situation into account.

Part of the magic of childhood lies in its diversity, both
within each child as he or she develops, and between children
at any given age. Despite that diversity, we can see clear
patterns in children's behaviors.

My friend Dr. T. Berry Brazelton, perhaps the world's fore-
most behavioral pediatrician, loves to tell stories of mothers
from the early days of his practice who, now that thirty or
more years have passed, tell him how remarkably accurate
his predictions were when he saw those children as infants.
To help parents anticipate and cope with later problems, soon
after their child's birth he would tell them that their child
would, around the age of two, become defiant and strong-
willed.

Although he intended it as a description of normal development—almost all children show signs of defiance when
they're about two years old—some parents interpreted his
statements as predictions based on something special in their
newborns' behavior. To them, it was as if he could magically
predict their children's future.

There are many such predictable patterns during the first
few years of life. We can, with great accuracy, tell parents
that their babies will learn to sit up, look for hidden objects,
and start to say a few words during the first year. We're much
less accurate if asked to describe *exactly when* a child will be
able to do any of those tasks.

Our margins of error increase as the child grows. We can
be much more sure of what a full-term baby will do during
the first three days after birth than during the three-hun-
dredth day.

Luckily, having a level of precision that would allow you

to predict which group of children will walk five days earlier than another group is unnecessary. In the long run it doesn't matter. Another pediatrician friend of mine, who has nine children of her own, told me she was so excited when her first son started walking early that she called up one of her old professors from medical school to find out if that might mean the boy was intellectually gifted. The professor listened to her gush with pride, and then said, "Of course, he may simply be a dumb jock." (The boy later became a physician.)

All parents pay attention to the obvious signs that their children are growing. We celebrate their first words and first steps, and share our joy with friends and relatives. But there are more subtle yet predictable signs of development which, if we look close enough, often tell us more about our children. Why do they cry in certain patterns? How do they learn to comfort themselves? What skills are they born with that soon disappear?

Child development is a remarkable process to watch, especially in our own children. The more information we have to give us a sense of perspective on what our children are doing—and why they are doing it at that particular stage of their lives—the more fascinating and magical it becomes. And the more we know, the more fun and less stressful raising our children can be.

Of course, no amount of knowledge or experience will make being a parent completely stress-free. A friend of mine, who's an internationally known psychologist and the director of a well-respected child development research center, once told me that when his children were little he would occasionally find himself yelling at them, "Grow up! Grow up!"

Even Dr. Benjamin Spock, the best-known and one of the most respected experts on child development, admits having had such feelings as a new parent.

I remember when I was a medical student, picking up my own crying six-month-old baby in the middle of the night and yelling, "Shut up!" at him, barely able to control myself from physically hurting him. He hadn't slept through the night for weeks, due to roseola followed by difficult teething, and his mother and I were exhausted and at our wits' end.[1]

So it's important that you not hold yourself to an impossibly high standard. Expect yourself to be angry and frustrated and just plain overwhelmed at times. Look for ways to channel those emotions without taking it out on your child, your spouse, or yourself. I'll get into some specifics later on in this book.

Child development is a popular topic. My shelves are filled with professional and technical books and journals on child development and psychology. (One of the benefits of being a columnist is that a lot of publishers send me books in the hope that I'll mention them in the newspapers or magazines. I receive more than a dozen new books of widely varying quality and relevance every week.)

Yet much of the information in professional publications is difficult for parents to interpret and apply to their own children. Academic psychology and psychiatry have a language all their own. (Some call it "psychobabble"—an unkind but accurate description of the unclear writing and confused thinking that permeate many books and articles in the field.) Too much writing about psychology is chock-full of seven-syllable compound nouns and sentences that run on for half a page. It's as if the authors believe that complexity is more professional and impressive than simplicity. In fact, the opposite is true.

This book, which is the second in a five-book series on child development and parent-child communication, is different. My goal, both in my *New York Times* "Parent & Child" column and in these books, is to provide parents with practical information and a sense of perspective. It is based on more than one thousand interviews I have done over the past few years with some of the world's finest psychologists, psychiatrists, pediatricians, and other experts. They are researchers, clinicians, teachers, and, more often than not, parents as well.

[1]B. Spock and M. B. Rothenberg, *Dr. Spock's Baby and Child Care* (New York: Pocket Books, 1992), p. 738.

This book is not meant to replace the popular works of such respected authors as Benjamin Spock, T. Berry Brazelton, Haim Ginott, or Penelope Leach. My own copies of their books are dog-eared from the many times I have turned to them, both as a psychologist and as a parent. Nor is the book a traditional academic treatise, filled with hundreds of footnotes and citations. Such annotation would simply get in the way of the typical new parent who, to put it bluntly, is more likely to read this book at two A.M. in the bathroom—for that is the only peaceful time he or she has for the first few months—than in an oak-paneled library. (That's one of the reasons why I've kept the chapters brief.)

Instead, I hope to take you on a journey inside the mind of your child. By viewing the world anew from a child's perspective, you can make sense of their often-cryptic behaviors. If you understand how children think during their various developmental stages—and you can spot the markers for those stages—then their specific "problem" behaviors will make more sense and be easier to handle.

I also hope to take you on an exploration of your own mind and feelings, especially during the times before and during pregnancy, and immediately after a child's birth. Most books for new parents pay little attention to how the thoughts we have in the months before birth influence how we respond to our newborn children.

That is why, unlike most books on infant development or parenting, we will begin the trip with a look at pregnancy and the period before pregnancy when we think about becoming parents. Instead of focusing on the biology of pregnancy and fetal development, which is covered so well in other books, we'll look at the emotions that accompany the transition to parenthood. We'll explore the often-uncomfortable feelings and fears we have during pregnancy that are perfectly normal, but seldom discussed. We'll examine the expectations, realistic and otherwise, we have for ourselves as parents. We'll look at childbirth not as the beginning of parenthood, but as part of a continuing process of becoming a parent.

We'll see how our generation's introduction to parenthood is different from preceding generations'.

As this book progresses, we will explore the reasons behind some of the things that puzzle and frustrate us the most about our children. What can my newborn child really do? What (and whom) does she already know? Why won't my baby stop crying in the evening? Why is she suddenly so picky about what she eats? Is it normal for me to get so angry with my baby?

To understand why infants behave certain ways, we have to look at the world through their eyes, without the assumptions and perspective we bring with us as adults. Sometimes that's best done by literally getting down on your hands and knees so that you can see things from their level. (In fact, it's a good idea to do precisely that when you're "baby-proofing" a room. You'll sometimes spot hazards and temptations that you missed when your eyes were five feet off the ground.)

More often, we can get information about how infants perceive and interpret their world by watching their behavior with trained eyes. Babies communicate how they are feeling from their first moments outside the womb. Their cries of pain and hunger are obvious to everyone. But if you watch very closely and know what to look for, newborns will tell you a great deal more. Are they overwhelmed by the lights and noises around them, or even by your touch? Do they know who you are? Do they want you to talk to them more softly?

The more attuned you are to those and other subtle communications that start even before your child is born, the better you will know your child. His or her behaviors will become more predictable and less frustrating. Your problems—and there are always many problems—will be easier to decipher and overcome.

It's important to remember that although psychology may be a science, raising children is not. *There's no one right way to raise children.* Part of the magic of childhood is the way some children from the dreariest or most frightening environments blossom into successful and caring adults.

Raising children is like an ever-changing family recipe that's modified by each generation, sometimes subtly, sometimes radically. As with all recipes, the best dishes are often created through our need to improvise on the spur of the moment.

Over the past decade I have noticed an unfortunate rekindling of the belief that every emotional or addiction problem an adult may have can be squarely blamed on his or her parents. That's simply not true. One of my favorite cartoons shows a huge auditorium with a banner over the seats reading ANNUAL MEETING: ADULT CHILDREN OF NORMAL PARENTS. There are only two or three people in the audience.

There is no doubt that, for example, having an alcoholic father or being raised by a single teenage mother can have profound lifelong effects. But all too often these days, parents are used as scapegoats by adults who wish to deny responsibility for their own actions. The irony of this belief is that it puts extraordinary and unnecessary pressures on these people when they become parents themselves. They worry about making even the slightest mistake that will "screw up their children." (Of course, there's a big difference between making a mistake, such as trying to toilet train your child before he's ready, and physically, sexually, or emotionally abusing that child.)

Being successful parents means that we must be willing to make mistakes—lots and lots of mistakes. A psychologist and professor of pediatrics I know wisely tells new parents that God allows them to make fifty thousand mistakes before they have to apply for a refill. He makes his point well, for too many new parents worry that they have to be perfect. That fear makes them dwell on their inevitable mistakes, when they really need to brush themselves off and move on.

To enjoy raising children, we must have the tools to recognize, understand, and recover from at least some of our mistakes so that we don't keep repeating them. One sign of a successful parent is that he or she makes many mistakes— but they are *new and improved mistakes* instead of repetitions of the old ones. One sign of a successful child is that he or she knows how to recover from a mistake. Knowing that they don't have to do everything perfectly, or even well, gives children the freedom to experiment, grow, and gain confidence in themselves. It is a powerful and precious gift that their parents can give them.

Although this book can be read from start to finish, please don't feel you have to use it that way. It is designed to be munched like a series of small snacks, which can be consumed in any order you wish. (Being an avid Chinese-food fan, I think of this as the *dim sum* approach to reading.) There is no single, all-encompassing chapter on the one-month-old or the six-month old. I've found that it's much more useful to look at the recurrent themes of pregnancy and childhood.

That's why I've often described child development as if it were a musical symphony. It is an elaboration of certain fundamental themes that appear over and over again in different guises. There are peaceful passages where the theme is clearly heard. But there are also stormy, cacophonous movements where the theme is deeply buried. Part of the challenge of being a parent is listening for those themes so that we can make better sense of our children's often-confusing emotions and behaviors.

The same can be said of our own emotions and relationships as adults during pregnancy, childbirth, and the first few years that follow. You need to understand the relationships you build with your children even before they are born, and the many ways, both subtle and obvious, becoming a parent affects your relationship with your spouse.

As with my *New York Times* column and my earlier book, I've tried to put the practical "what can I do about this" information in boxes scattered throughout the chapters. I've also added some charts and questionnaires you may wish to fill out to help keep track of how you and your baby are changing, and what you are feeling. Unless I specifically mention sex differences, everything I write about girls applies equally to boys, and vice versa. I have tried to use "he" and "she" at random and without bias.

Being a parent is probably the most stressful job you'll

ever undertake. It's also the most rewarding. The more you understand about your children, the more fun and exciting it will be to share their lives. Certainly no book, including this one, can help you cope with all the problems you'll face as a parent. Even the "best" kid can, at times, try the patience of a saint. (I tell people that all the things my son did as an infant that annoyed, frustrated, or infuriated me were things that, from the standpoint of child development, I wanted him to do. *I just didn't want him to do them to me, or at those particular moments!*)

As I've said in my articles and in my previous book, raising children is too serious a task to take seriously all the time. We must have the ability to laugh both with our children and at ourselves. And we must keep our sense of perspective. During my moments of greatest frustration as a parent I take comfort from two thoughts:

(1) Children are extremely resilient. We can make lots of mistakes and still wind up with wonderful kids. Neither we nor they have to be perfect.

(2) Our species successfully raised children for tens of thousands of years before the first person wrote down the word "psychology." The fundamental skills needed to be a parent are within us. All we're really doing is fine-tuning a process that's already remarkably successful.

PREGNANCY AND YOUR BABY'S FIRST YEAR

CHAPTER 1

Preparing for Parenthood

I realized when I was pregnant that it was the first situation in
my life I couldn't talk my way out of.
—A FRIEND, WHO NOW HAS TWO CHILDREN

THE VIEW FROM OUR MIND'S EYE

Our children exist in our minds before they are conceived in
our bodies. We envision them only vaguely at first. They are
reflections of our own past, either as it actually was or as we
would like it to have been. Our imagined children giggle and
coo and, after a blur of time, trot off to school with smiles on
their glowing faces. They hit home runs and have the lead
roles in plays. They bring us pride and attention from our
friends and relatives. They poignantly tell us they love us—
which is what we most want to hear.

We also recall long-forgotten memories from our own childhood. The images and emotions are surprisingly vivid as we
remember being taunted by a neighborhood bully or riding a
bicycle for the first time. We once again feel the family tensions
from long ago, and apply them to our own growing family.
Will we do well enough financially? What if we become ill?

But soon after the decision to have a child or the realization that one is on the way, a different image sometimes invades our consciousness. We begin to notice the babies who are imperfect. We become acutely aware of the ones who are deformed or crippled or mentally retarded. We pay close and painful attention to the stories of babies who are born ill or who die. And we become frightened and feel as if we are alone.

What have we gotten ourselves into? How can we possibly cope if our baby is born with something seriously wrong? We worry about our strength to live with a child whose demands are interminable or who is, from the beginning, fighting a losing battle for life. And in the quiet moments of the night's darkness, we wonder about the things that frighten us the most: pain, death, and abandonment.

Most of the times that I've spoken with prospective parents, I've seen these fears lurking beneath the surface. All too often they are emotions that they've kept to themselves out of fear or embarrassment or confusion, not even daring to share them with their spouses. They worry that their feelings and concerns are a sign that something is wrong. It is as if giving voice to their deepest fears might make them come true.

Yet the truth is the exact opposite. Prospective parents who share these disturbing thoughts often find that their spouses have been going through exactly the same thing, also afraid to talk. Their unspoken fears have created a barrier between them as each, with the best of intentions, tries to protect the other by denying what he or she needs most: a feeling of support.

The occasionally vivid and frightening images of our children-to-be are actually a sign of maturity and, perhaps, parental competence. They are a way for the prospective mother and father to test their ability to face the unthinkable. They are also an opportunity to reinforce the bonds between couples and families as we search for strength.

Whenever I've spoken to pregnant girls in their early teens, I've been struck by their unrealistic appraisal of their situations, and of how having a child will profoundly affect all aspects of their lives. Again and again I've heard them say the words that tell me how ill-prepared they are to be parents: "Now I'll have someone who'll love me forever." They are looking in vain to their unborn children for what they had hoped for from their own parents.

The fantasies of these pregnant teenagers, who are little more than children themselves, tell us how much they need to learn about their babies. They envision only that first mythological child—the one who is all giggles and coos and adoration. They are not emotionally prepared for even the most ordinary stresses they will face as the parents of healthy, normal babies: the sleepless nights and the power struggles, the worries about money and chicken pox and school grades. They are even less prepared for the predictable problems of the underweight, high-risk babies they all-too-often carry.

One of the most innovative school-based programs to help young adolescents understand some of the realities of parenthood involves what are known as "flour babies." Although the details may vary, the fundamental concept of the program involves pairing boys and girls into couples, and giving them a ten-pound sack of flour to care for. Even though the flour obviously doesn't require any feeding or changing, the "parents" still have to look after it all day and all night, at home and at school for about a week.

That means they can't go to a movie or an after-school job, or do anything else for that matter, without either lugging the sack with them or arranging for a baby-sitter. All of a sudden, the constant demands of even the most obedient baby become much more apparent to the prospective mother or father. The teenagers have to negotiate with each other over who gets to go where alone, and who's left with the "baby."

It's really a brilliant idea, because it taps into the adolescents' developmental stage. Teenagers learn best by experiencing things themselves. They simply don't believe adults who tell them how exhausting being a parent is. In fact, by telling adolescents, "You're not old enough yet," you're challenging them to prove you wrong.

The flour-baby programs take the opposite approach by offering adolescents safe ways of experiencing some aspects of what parenthood is like. The fourteen-year-old who says to herself, "Well, it wouldn't be like that for me. I can handle it," suddenly finds herself overwhelmed by the intricacies of caring for a bag of flour—let alone a real baby.

Most adult new parents, however, underestimate their skills at caring for children. When Dr. Benjamin Spock wrote *Baby and Child Care*—the book that became the bible for American parents in the middle of the twentieth century—he wisely began with some much-needed words of reassurance: "Trust yourself. You know more than you think you do."

◆   ◆   ◆

A LOOK AT OUR EXPECTATIONS

If you or your partner is pregnant or thinking about becoming pregnant, take a few minutes to complete the statements below. Although you should feel free to use more than one answer for each if you'd like, try to be brief and focused. If there are other people you feel close to, such as your own parents or siblings, you can ask them to complete these statements with reference to you and your forthcoming baby.

The best way to do this exercise is for each of you to write your answers on separate sheets of paper without consulting each other. I've enclosed in parentheses some possible answers for all but the last question, but don't limit yourself to what I've written down. Instead, use those ideas to stimulate your own thinking and to explore areas you may not have consciously considered.

Remember, there are no right answers. Try to be as honest as you can.

◆ When I think about pregnancy, I feel _____.
(Frightened? Proud? Giddy? Grown up? Too young? Too old?)

♦ I want my child to be _____. (A girl/boy? Attractive? Brilliant? Tall? Successful? Happy? Normal? An athlete? Rich? Everything I couldn't be? Good at things I'm bad at?)

♦ I worry that my child will be _____. (Retarded? Deformed? A girl/boy? Ordinary? Mentally ill? Physically ill? A failure? An embarrassment? An interference in my life?)

♦ I'd be more comfortable with a girl/boy (choose one) because _____. (That's what I am? That's what I'm not? I think it would be easier for me? I think it would be easier for her/him?)

♦ The things I think I'll do best as a parent are _____. (Day-to-day care? Listen to problems? Teach? Discipline? What my own parents did best?)

♦ The things I think I'll do worst as a parent are _____. (Day-to-day care? Keeping my temper? Discipline? Play? Handling crises?)

♦ As a parent, I'll be most comfortable with _____. (The physical care of my child? Teaching my child new things? Sharing my own childhood experiences?)

♦ As a parent, I'll be least comfortable with _____. (The physical care of my child? Discipline? Returning to work? Leaving my job? Thinking of myself as a mom/dad?)

♦ The best thing that could happen during the pregnancy would be _____. (For everything to go like clockwork? For me to go into labor a few weeks early? For my spouse to change his/her behavior toward me?)

♦ The worst thing that could happen during the pregnancy would be _____. (For me to lose this baby? To discover that something's wrong with my baby? For my spouse to think of me as less attractive? For my spouse to leave me?)

♦ If my baby is physically or mentally disabled, I will _____. (Cope with it? Break down? Be very angry at myself? Be very angry at my spouse? Feel responsible?)

♦ If my baby dies, I will _____. (Never have another child? Try to have another child immediately? Believe it was for the best?)

♦ During the pregnancy I expect my partner to _____. (Pay more attention to me? Pay less attention to me? Prepare for how our lives will change? Have a lower/higher interest in sex?)

♦ During the pregnancy I expect myself to _____. (Be uncomfortable? Have more time to myself? Fall in love with my new baby? Worry about the future? Feel fat? Feel beautiful?)

♦ During labor and delivery I expect my partner to _____. (If you're a woman: Be with me the whole time? Hold my hand? Ease my pain? Leave me alone? If you're a man: Scream and yell? Be in a lot of pain? Not to tell me when it hurts?)

♦ During labor and delivery I expect myself to _____. (Be strong? Be frightened? Hurt a lot? Take it all in stride? Feel embarrassed?)

♦ During my baby's first few weeks of life I expect my partner to _____. (Take primary responsibility for caring for our child? Back me up when I can't care for our child? Take time off from work? Take care of organizing things?)

♦ During my baby's first few weeks of life I expect myself to _____. (Be exhausted? Be exhilarated? Spend a lot of time with my child?)

♦ I'll be happy if _____.

♦   ♦   ♦

You can use this quiz as a springboard for gaining more insight into your own feelings and for discussing your hopes, worries, and expectations with the important people around you. Several of the questions are purposely ambiguous. As you compare your answers, look at whether you and your partner are focusing on different issues.

For example, when answering what you hope your child will be, did you write down an answer relating to the child's health, financial security, physical appearance, intellectual ability, emotions, or something else? Are most of your fears surrounding pregnancy focused on pain, failure, embarrassment, competition with other family members, or something else? Which of your hopes, fears, and expectations are shared by your partner? How are your answers different from your partner's?

Perhaps most important, you can use this quiz as a step toward figuring out how you can work together to handle your concerns. How can you help each other prevent the things you fear? Who's going to get up at two A.M. when your baby cries?

You'll probably find that there are quite a few areas where you and your partner have different hopes, fears, and expectations for yourselves, each other, and your baby. Don't worry about that; it's perfectly normal. By becoming aware of and discussing your differences, you'll be better prepared to face the challenges of being parents together.

It's easy, when you do an exercise like this, to get caught up in all the negative thoughts and fears. Pregnancy represents one of the great unknowns in life. Everyone's at least a little worried about how it will turn out. Be sure to take some time toward the end of your discussion with your partner to focus on the things that excite you about being a parent.

Indulge your fantasies a bit. Think back to the special moments from the first few years of your own childhood: learning to ride a bicycle or to tie your shoes, feeding the ducks at a pond or the pigeons at a park, opening presents on your birthday or a holiday. Now imagine yourself doing that with your new child, and bask in the images. Those times will soon come.

THE PREGNANT RELATIONSHIP

We usually don't think of relationships as being pregnant. Yet the impending birth of a child often has profound effects on the way we interact with those closest to us. Pregnant women may feel both excited and upset by the changes their bodies are undergoing.

Men may have difficulty viewing their partners both as mothers and as sexual beings. It's a reflection of the ambivalent feelings we have about our own parents' sexuality. In some families these two problems feed on each other. The man has difficulty becoming sexually aroused as his partner begins to show her pregnancy. The woman, who's already concerned about the attractiveness of her changing body, interprets this as a rejection and feels even less attractive.

The other physical and biochemical changes only make things worse. As the pregnancy progresses, the growing fetus puts pressure on the woman's internal organs. (My wife describes the last few weeks of pregnancy as going from feeling that you're out of breath to feeling that you're out of bladder.) The added weight can cause back and foot pains as well.

Many pregnant women find themselves becoming more emotional as new levels of hormones course through their bodies. (I'll have more on these emotional changes in a later chapter.) They may become acutely depressed, both before and after their children are born. These women often don't want to get out of bed. They may feel unable to sleep or may sleep excessively. They may cry with little apparent provocation. Most of the time this type of depression goes away by itself. Even so, it's a good idea to mention it to your physician.

Although the "baby blues" (postpartum depression) are common during the first few weeks after giving birth, a very small number of women become psychotic and may even hear voices telling them to kill their babies. (Before you get too worried, remember that it's a *very* small number of women. Also, the problem tends to run in families. If your mother or other close family members were severely depressed after giving birth, it's a good idea to tell both your partner and your physician.)

It's easy for men to misinterpret their partners' emotional outbursts. If the man feels he should be providing for his partner's well-being, he'll tend to interpret her yelling or crying as an indication that he has failed. If he's nervous and unsure of what his new role as a father will be like, he may see her outbursts as a challenge to his competence, and will yell back. Neither of these responses will help the situation.

Instead, it's important to remember that the woman's increased emotionality may be due to something beyond her control, and beyond the control of her partner. This doesn't mean that a pregnant woman's feelings should be dismissed or ignored. Rather, for the relationship to survive the occasional hormonal storms, both partners have to recognize and understand what's going on. It may help to see these rapid emotional swings as preparation for the stresses and joys of the months that follow your child's birth.

◆   ◆   ◆

MAKE TOUGH DECISIONS EARLY

With all the dreaming, worrying, and shopping that go on during pregnancy, it's easy to overlook some decisions that parents are best off discussing before their children are born. This doesn't mean that all is lost if you haven't reached decisions during pregnancy. Rather, these are complex issues that may take a lot of thinking and talking to resolve.

◆ How much time will each of you take off from work, both before and after your baby is born? Parental leave—especially parental leave for fathers and for adoptive parents—is an unfamiliar concept in the United States. (The failure of the federal government to mandate unpaid parental leave with job protection is a disgrace! Many other countries require employers to offer such a program because they recognize the special importance of the parent-child relationship in the first few months.)

Keep in mind that most first-time parents underestimate how tired they will be during the first year after their child is born. This is especially true during the first few days at home, now that insurance companies are keeping healthy mothers and their newborns in the hospital for only a day or two. You might wish to consider arranging for someone to "take the night shift" for the first few days you're at home so that someone else can change your baby, feed her from a bottle or bring her to you for breast feedings, and generally keep an eye on her while the two of you recuperate from your ordeal.

If you have an experienced relative who will help you with this, that's great. (That's also a very generous relative.) Otherwise, home nursing services will arrange for someone who has experience with newborns to help you out. It's expensive, but well worth it.

♦ If both of you will be returning to work, talk about how you will do so. Will one or both of you go back to a part-time job? Will you be sharing a job with someone else?

If you're going to go back to full-time work, try not to start on a Monday. It will be easier to adjust if you have a weekend break after only two or three days back on the job. Don't expect that you'll be able to resume work at your former pace. You'll be too sleep-deprived and have so many new things on your mind. The same goes for any cooking or housecleaning you do. Expect to order more takeout food, to warm up more frozen dinners, and to let the dirt and the laundry pile up more than usual for at least a few months.

♦ Look into the child-care options available to you. It's important that you think of it as "child care," not as "day care." This is more than a matter of semantics. It's an orientation toward the job. Calling it *child care* means that you're emphasizing the treatment of the child. Calling it *day care* shows that the emphasis is on the passage of time. I'll discuss ways of evaluating and selecting a child-care provider later in this book.

There are many types of child care, varying in both style and expense. Will you be relying on a relative to care for your child? Will you be bringing someone into your home? Will you be forming a cooperative with a group of other parents? Will you be using a family child-care provider or a large child-care center?

Each of these can be very successful, both for you and for your child. The one approach that almost always fails, even though parents still try it, hoping to beat the odds, is working at home while caring for your child. According to Dr. Kathleen Christensen, the director of the National Project on Home-Based Work at the City University of New York Graduate School, you still need some child care help if you're going to accomplish anything in your job. You can't expect to rock the cradle with your foot while you operate a computer or sewing machine with your hands.

In her national survey of women who worked at home,[1] Dr. Christensen found that those who had young children and no help caring for them were exhausted. They often worked until two A.M. and then got up with their family a few hours later. The hours after their children fell asleep were the only time they could get any of their work done.

If you choose any approach to child care other than a large center, look into backups for the times when the person you're counting on is sick or takes a vacation or even decides to leave the business. Few things are more frustrating than having to find someone to care for your child at the last moment.

♦ Talk about how you envision your child's religious upbringing. This is important not only for families where the parents are of different religions, but for those where they've had similar upbringings.

[1]K. Christensen, *Women and Home-Based Work: The Unspoken Contract* (New York: Henry Holt, 1988), p. 136.

If your child is a boy, will he be circumcised? What about baptisms and other religious ceremonies? Many of these decisions have to be made soon after your child is born. Since you won't be thinking very clearly then, you should plan for them.

Sometimes parents are surprised by their spouses' ideas about children's religious education. A father who seldom attends a church or synagogue may wish his child to have more religious instruction. A mother who was raised in a devout family may hope her child has a different experience growing up. In any event, it's best to broach the subject long before you or your child has to make any formal decisions.

♦   ♦   ♦

CHAPTER 2

When Your Pregnancy Is "Different"

The essence of parenting does not lie in what one does for one's baby, but rather in the exchange, in the intensely rewarding feedback one can establish between the baby and oneself. The different ways to achieve this exchange are numerous and highly individualized.

—T. BERRY BRAZELTON, M.D.[1]

There is a remarkable and wonderful diversity among families. Yet those who don't fit their preconceived images of what they should be as a new parent (young, fertile, financially successful, or whatever) feel awkward, as if they are somehow breaking unwritten rules. They worry that they must fit a particular mold if they are to raise a child successfully.

Our idealized images of successful parents are filled with contradictions. We expect them (and therefore ourselves) to be young—but not too young. They must be mature as well. We want them to be financially secure—but not working long hours to achieve that security. We expect them to be loving and devoted, but not smothering and all-absorbed with their child. Such a vision is impossible to achieve.

Yet many "atypical" parents (and I use that phrase with

[1]T. B. Brazelton, *On Becoming a Family* (New York: Dell, 1981), p. xiii.

great hesitation since I'm not sure what a "typical" parent is) have a nagging worry that they are fundamentally different from the parents of their mythology. Let's take a look at some of the most common variations: older parents, adoptive parents, and stepparents who have a new baby. It's also important to think about another variation of pregnancy: one that results in a stillbirth, miscarriage, or abortion. Those parents will, both at the same time and during later pregnancies, have some very strong emotions to contend with.

BEING AN OLDER PARENT

"We have more wisdom and less stamina than younger parents. It's a trade-off," said a woman I interviewed who was thirty-nine years old when she had her first child and forty-two when she had her second. She is one of a significant number of adults who become parents at an age when many of their contemporaries are worrying about paying their children's college tuition.

Although many recent articles in newspapers and magazines would have you believe that the trend toward older parents is new, it is not. The latest census figures in the United States show that there were fewer births to women over forty in 1987 (the most recent year analyzed) than in any year from 1950 to 1965. There were also fewer first children born to mothers over forty in 1987 than there were in each of the years from 1950 to 1955.

The number of older parents in the last half of the twentieth century (as well as the growing number of young teenage mothers) reflect biological changes in response to both nutrition and economics. Over the past one hundred years, the average age of menarche in the United States (the age at which a woman has her first menstrual period) has been dropping at the rate of three to four months every decade. That means that a teenager today is physically able to reproduce about three and a half years earlier than her great-great-grandmother probably could. This seems to be a function of better overall nutrition—the same reason people are, on average, taller than they were a century ago.

While biological changes are making it possible for younger adolescents to bear children, on average, couples today are getting married and having children later than in previous generations. This appears to reflect economic changes, especially the growth over the past one hundred years in the proportion of women entering higher education and holding jobs outside the home. Since women, on average, become less fertile as they enter their thirties, those who wait until they are older to try to have children also tend to take longer to become pregnant.

Many older parents are concerned about the effect their ages might have on their relationships with their children. They worry about sticking out. Will their children be ashamed of them because of their age? Will they feel awkward at school functions? Will they become medically or financially dependent on their children?

While children of older parents often report feeling acutely aware of their parents' ages, many feel that the advantages of having older parents outweigh the disadvantages. Older parents tend to be more secure financially and able to spend more time with their children than younger parents.

One twenty-seven-year-old woman I interviewed had a father who was fifty-three and a mother who was forty-one when she was born. "They didn't choose to be older parents," she said. "They simply chose to be parents. It's just that they got married later in life."

◆ ◆ ◆

TIPS FOR OLDER PARENTS

When my son was a month or so "behind schedule" for getting his first teeth, I asked a dentist if I should be concerned. He wisely looked at me and said there was no point in worrying. After all, what could I *do* about it?

In many respects, the same could be said about being

an older-than-average parent. Since there's no way you can make yourself younger, why worry about it?

You should, of course, get thorough prenatal care, just like any expectant mother. You should also talk to your physician about certain tests for birth defects, such as amniocentesis (using a long, thin needle to withdraw some of the amniotic fluid that surrounds your baby) or chorionic villus sampling (removing a tiny piece of the placenta through a tube). Both of these can spot certain genetic and other problems fairly early in the pregnancy.

Remember that your newborn baby won't care how old you are. She's more concerned with the really important things, like how much you'll feed and cuddle her. Besides, by the time she reaches grade school, she'll have a distorted sense of age anyway. Anyone over the age of fifteen will seem ancient to her, no matter how old you really are.

Some new but older biological parents may already be stepparents through their spouse's previous marriage. This can lead to some complex but manageable situations. I'll have an entire section on that in a few pages.

◆   ◆   ◆

ADOPTING A CHILD

There are about sixty thousand adoptions by adults unrelated to their children each year in the United States, ten thousand of which are international adoptions. The reasons for adopting children are multifold, and include infertility, concern about passing on a genetic problem, or simply the desire to care for some children who need a good family.

As someone who was adopted at birth and who has conducted psychological research on adoption, I've always had a strong interest in this area. The more I've looked into it, the more I've been struck by the mixed messages our culture gives everyone in the adoption triad—the birth parents, the adoptive parents, and the children.

With one breath, we tell people that adoption is a noble act. The children are "chosen." The birth parents are "self-less." The adoptive parents are "virtuous" or even "saintly."

But in the next breath, we wonder what was wrong with those children, that they have been given up for adoption. We belittle the birth parents, especially the mothers, for being stupid enough to get pregnant in the first place. We question their morals and their motives. Most painful are the assumptions about and comments to the adoptive parents. What is wrong with them that they had to make this "second-best" choice? Are they really sure they can't have a child of their own? Once they adopt, they'll immediately get pregnant because the pressure will be off!

Both these extremes are wrong, of course. There is nothing inherently more noble in being an adoptive parent than a biological parent. Adoptive parents get just as angry with and frustrated by their children. They also get the same pleasures and benefits that other parents get. But labeling them as noble does prospective adoptive parents a disservice, since it may make them feel that they ought to be infallible or even saintly instead of simply human.

Nor is there anything "second-best" or "unnatural" about wanting to care for a child who isn't related to you. Whether you're able to conceive a child on your own is completely irrelevant to whether you can care for one in the years that follow. Besides, it's really no one else's business. To imply, by saying that a woman will become pregnant as soon as she adopts, that the couple's infertility was "all in their heads," is cruel. It also flies in the face of what we now know about the intricacies of reproductive biology.

The women who give up their children for adoption don't fit into a few simple categories either. For most, it is a very difficult and well thought-out decision. Whether they choose to give up their babies because they don't feel ready to be mothers; they're already overwhelmed with other children in their family; they don't believe in elective abortion; or some other reason—is immaterial.

And the children are children. While they may statistically be more likely, in the United States at least, than the average child to be of mixed-race parentage, to have a physical disability or illness, or to join your family when they are older— they are fundamentally children, not adoptees. You can't tell an adopted baby's cry from that of any other baby. Nor can you tell them apart when they smile.

Prospective adoptive parents are often shocked by how differently they are treated from other adults. Unlike most parents, they have to justify to social workers and, even occasionally to the biological mother, their motivations for caring for a child. While there are valid reasons for screening adoptive parents, many who go through the process say it feels like it's a cross between a job interview, a loan application, and being back in the second grade.

Do you tell the adoption agency the truth, or the things you think they would like to hear? Will you be rejected if you say you only want a baby who isn't physically or mentally disabled? Should you express your concerns about raising a child who is from another culture or of a different race?

Unfortunately, there are no simple answers to these questions. Although it's generally a good idea to be honest with the agency about your concerns and preferences, there are times when some sensitivity to the internal politics of the agencies will help you out.[2]

It's also a good idea to get involved with an adoption support group, such as Adoptive Families of America.[3] This is

[2]When my parents were looking to adopt a child in the early 1950s, they approached several agencies. When the application forms asked about their religion, they honestly (but naïvely) wrote down "atheist." Because of that, no agency would give them a baby.

[3]Their national headquarters is located at 3333 Highway 100 North, Minneapolis, MN 55422; phone (612) 535-4829. They also have a few hundred local chapters throughout the country.

especially true if you're adopting a child from another culture or of another race, or a "special needs" child who has a physical or mental disability. With these children, it's tougher to get the advice and support you need from your family, friends, and neighbors.

◆   ◆   ◆

THE MYTHOLOGY OF ADOPTION

Adoption of various sorts is a universal theme in children's literature. Every child wonders, at times, if he is really a prince who was kidnapped at birth, or if she is the missing heiress of a wealthy and respected family. Our own parents—biological, adoptive, or step—pale by comparison to these imaginary families.

As an adoptive parent, it's important to take a second look at the fairy tales and myths we enjoyed as children, for they helped mold our subconscious adult perceptions of adoption. That's because the adoption theme in so many stories serves a very important role in early development.

By identifying with the adopted characters in these stories, children get to express feelings that are too threatening to express directly. A child who's angry at her siblings or parents, but confused and perhaps frightened by her anger, will take great joy in listening to such stories as "Cinderella." A child who feels unloved or exploited may live out her fantasies through "Rapunzel."

But what should you feel now that your role is sometimes portrayed as the wicked stepmother or the witch who absconded with the baby? Do you feel at some level that being an adoptive parent dooms you to eventual rejection and failure?

It's interesting to see how children from different cultures integrate the theme of adoption into their lives. My mother, who was raised in Russia and Romania until she was ten, used to tell me that whenever she was upset at her family, she became convinced that she had been kidnapped by Gypsies. Someday, she thought as a young child, her real parents would find her so that she could lead the life of luxury to which she was entitled.

A friend of mine, who was raised in China, distinctly recalls the times when her mother was very upset with her. The mother expressed her anger by telling her daughter that she was adopted. "I'm not your real mother," she would say. "I found you on a park bench and brought you home."

My friend found this terrifying. At the same time, it helped her make sense of her jealous feelings toward her brother, who was clearly their mother's favorite.

So take an evening or two to reread some of the stories you enjoyed listening to as a child. You'll see them from a very different perspective.

◆   ◆   ◆

THE NEW BABY IN A STEPFAMILY

I once interviewed a woman who said that it took her a few minutes to fully describe the biological and legal links among the children in her life. A large chart would have helped, too. She had brought two children from a previous marriage into her current one. Her current husband brought three children from his earlier marriage. They had two children together. Her ex-husband also remarried and had a child by his second wife. Her family tree was as complex as the list of characters in a Russian novel.

A growing number of first-time biological parents are already stepparents. For them and for their spouses, deciding to have a child together triggers different concerns. They wonder how it will affect their biological children from previous relationships, their stepchildren, and their current marriage.

All of this can add tremendous stress to the pregnancy. In

order to make the most of your relationship with the new baby, it's very important to understand what your older children or stepchildren are probably feeling. Researchers who have studied these families have discovered some interesting patterns that aren't intuitively obvious.

Much of the time, the new baby brings a sense of closeness to all the family members. "All of a sudden everyone is related to each other," recalled one mother who'd done it.

But that closeness is less likely to occur if the new child arrives less than two or three years after the wedding. The normal feelings of jealousy and anxiety children have over the birth of a sibling are compounded by their adjustment to the stepfamily. They may feel as if the new child is more entitled than they are to a privileged position in the new family.

In one study of these families by Dr. Ann C. Bernstein,[4] she found that the children who had the most difficulty coping with a new sibling were between the ages of six and nine, had been their parents' only or youngest child, and were in stepfamilies where the birth took place within four years of the remarriage.

◆   ◆   ◆

TIPS FOR BLENDED FAMILIES

There are a few things that family therapists have found help your biological and stepchildren adjust during your pregnancy to the idea of having a new sibling. If you're in this situation, try to keep them in mind.

◆ Pay attention to how you refer to the forthcoming or new baby. Referring to her as "your half sister" instead of "your sister" will promote a feeling of divisiveness and alienation among the other children in your family.

◆ Try to involve all the children in your family in

[4] A. C. Bernstein, *Yours, Mine, and Ours: How Families Change When Remarried Parents Have a Child Together* (New York: Scribner's, 1989).

preparations for and care of your new baby. This is especially important for children who aren't living with you.
If, for example, your husband's son is living primarily
with his biological mother, it's easy to forget to get him
involved. But if you don't include him, he may come to
the conclusion that since Daddy has a new wife and a
new child, he doesn't need his "old" son anymore.

♦ Be sensitive to issues surrounding the new child's
last name. Children can sometimes be distressed that the
new child's last name is the same as some of theirs, but
not all of theirs. Because of this, those children who have
a different last name may not feel as close to the baby
as their stepsiblings do.

This is, of course, a problem not easily solved. Having
everyone change to the last name of the father in the
stepfamily may leave the stepchildren feeling like they
no longer are connected to their biological father. That
can lead to even more difficulties.

Open discussions before the baby is born can help
avoid some of the problems. Hyphenating the new
child's last name so that it combines the last names of
the other children might help. In fact, sometimes all the
children decide that they want the new hyphenated last
name, too. For them, it's a sign that they see their family
as stable, which is quite a compliment.

♦ ♦ ♦

MISCARRIAGES, ABORTIONS, AND STILLBIRTHS

We give parents confusing and sometimes cruel messages if
their pregnancies do not result in a living child. We do not
acknowledge the intensity and extent of their grief—feelings
that often surprise them as much as outsiders.

Yet the overwhelming nature of their grieving underscores
the emotional relationship they have built with their unborn

child. The knowledge that a miscarriage or stillbirth probably indicates that there was something seriously wrong with the child's development is of little comfort. Nor does voluntarily deciding to seek an abortion make parents immune to sometimes overwhelming feelings. They have bonded with and are grieving for the child who was in their mind's eye. They have lost a part of themselves.

Ironically, this intense grief is a reflection of greatly improved public health. It's common in cultures that have a high infant mortality rate for parents not to be as emotionally involved with their newborns. They may even delay naming the child for weeks or months, thereby delaying their recognition of her individuality until the period of highest risk has passed and the child has the odds of survival in her favor. It's a subtle, protective mechanism for the parents, for it spares them some of the grief they'd feel if they felt close to a baby who soon died.

Many times I've heard the fraction-of-a-second hesitation in a mother's voice when she's asked how many children she's had. That small pause is an homage to an unnamed but not forgotten child who was never born.

Friends and relatives will console parents who've had a miscarriage or stillbirth with well-meaning words of encouragement that they can surely have another child. But by treating the unborn child as an object which, like a broken vase, can be replaced, they are ignoring the relationship that had begun to form.

The parents' relationship with an aborted fetus—especially one which the mother chose to abort—is also mostly ignored. The thought of a voluntary abortion makes many people uncomfortable, even those who strongly support abortion on demand. A mother who decides to have an abortion still feels some emotional connection to that child and will, in her own way, grieve for it.

The messages too many of these mothers receive from others is that their feelings and sense of connection to that fetus must be forgotten. It's as if the pregnant woman's decision should be purely political and unemotional. But there is nothing inconsistent about wishing to terminate a pregnancy and grieving for the unborn child.

Some women repress their grief until they become pregnant with a baby they wish to bear. For them, the feelings they held back for so long can quickly become overwhelming. They begin to calculate how old their other children would have been, and what they might be doing now. They ponder the images and feel the emotions that they had denied themselves during the earlier pregnancy. It is all part of a healing process. It is a coming to terms with their new role as mother.

There's been a growing recognition among health-care professionals and clergy that parents of miscarried, aborted, and stillborn children must have their emotions and grief acknowledged. Some parents take great comfort in naming and holding funerals for their unborn or stillborn children. Doing so allows them to move on more smoothly with their lives, and to develop stronger relationships with any other children they may have.

One way to seek help with this, especially if you're feeling overwhelmed, is to contact a local children's hospital about a grief support group. Most will either have one that they run, or will refer you to one in your community. These groups can also be very useful for your partner if he or she doesn't understand why you're feeling so distraught.

The Other Pregnancy

My father's experience as a new parent seems to be fairly typical of his generation. During my mother's labor with me, he was out pacing the street in front of the hospital. When my grandfather finally came bearing the news that I was born, the two of them went out to celebrate, getting drunk together at a local bar.

—MARTIN GREENBERG, M.D.[1]

In many ways, the role of the father during pregnancy, labor, and delivery has changed dramatically over the past twenty-five years. The fathers of our parents' generation were expected to be passive observers. They were barred from prenatal examinations and the delivery room. There was something mysterious—almost religious and uncomfortably sexual—about the relationship between a woman and her obstetrician. It was an area into which the father dared not tread during the pregnancy for fear of learning what he should not (and should not want to) know.

Immediately after the birth, fathers were treated as unwelcome visitors while their wives, who had been sedated or anesthetized during the delivery, recovered from their ordeal. Fathers had to obey strict visiting hours, which implied that

[1] M. Greenberg, "Fathers: Falling in Love With Your Newborn," in *Experts Advise Parents*, ed. E. Shiff (New York: Delacorte, 1987), p. 27.

their presence was a detriment or at best an inconvenience to their wives and to the hospital staff.

They usually first viewed their children, all swaddled and labeled, through a nursery window smudged with the hand and nose prints of other fathers. If they asked to hold their newborn babies, they were politely but firmly told, "No. You're not sterile." (I've always loved the double meaning of that word when used in this context. Did the nurses, who felt very protective toward their newborn charges, mean that he was dirty and might infect them—something that could be quickly and easily remedied with some soap and water, a gown, and a mask? Or did they, at some deeper level, mean that he was sexually potent and, therefore, a threat to the baby's purity and innocence?)

It's no wonder that so many men of previous generations felt awkward about touching their newborn children. Many of the messages they had received over the months and years before the birth told them they were unneeded, incompetent, or contaminated. For them, being parents started sometime after their wives and children arrived back home. The relatively recent acceptance of men as an integral part of pregnancy, labor, and delivery has dramatically changed how they make their transitions to fatherhood.

THE EXPECTANT FATHER

There are hundreds of books that purport to tell women what to expect during their pregnancies. Yet I have only found one book[2] that focuses exclusively on what it feels like to be a pregnant father. There are, of course, vast physiological differences between what men and women go through during a pregnancy. But researchers have only recently begun to study how pregnancy affects men.

I used to watch the reaction when I told my friends that,

[2] J. L. Shapiro, When Men Are Pregnant (San Luis Obispo, CA: Impact Publishers, 1987).

during the first trimester of my wife's pregnancy with our son, I gained ten pounds and she stayed the same weight. After they laughed (for my friends are nothing if not polite), many of the men would tell similar stories of their own. One had developed strange cravings for food. Another had back pains and morning sickness. A third felt like his bladder had shrunk— for, like his wife, he was always running off to the bathroom.

Dr. Jerrold Lee Shapiro, a psychologist at the University of Santa Clara in California, has studied men during their wives' pregnancies and found that over 60 percent reported symptoms like these—problems they had expected to see in their wives, not in themselves. In fact, Dr. Shapiro admits to having gained thirty pounds during each of his wife's two pregnancies.

Physicians tend to dismiss these symptoms, often with a wisecrack that implies that fathers have no business feeling that way. A man who suffers these symptoms often responds to them with embarrassed humor. Yet neither would treat nausea or pain that way if the circumstances were different. The fact that such "sympathy pains" are so common may tell us that, at an unconscious level, men are trying to feel that they are a part of the pregnancy.

Our culture makes us uncomfortable with the idea that a man should feel anything except tenderness and anxiety during a pregnancy. But anthropologists and others who have studied childbirth in different cultures have found a wide range of beliefs about what men are expected to feel, not only during pregnancy, but during labor and delivery as well. At the extreme are those cultures that practice couvade: childbirth in which the father feels pain during the delivery, but the mother may not.

Dr. Ronald Melzack, a physiological psychologist at McGill University in Montreal and an expert on pain, has vividly described couvade:

> In some of these cultures a woman who is going to give birth continues to work in the fields until the child is just about to be born. Her husband then gets into bed and groans as though he were in great pain while she bears the child. In more ex-

treme cases, the husband stays in bed with the baby to recover from the terrible ordeal, and the mother almost immediately returns to attend to the crops.[3]

This magical sharing of the pain of childbirth was written about as far back as the first century A.D. and as recently as this century. Anthropologists have described it in cultures throughout much of the world, including those in North and South America, Europe, and Asia. (It's been least reported in Africa and Australia.) To this day, physicians and psychologists often label the nausea, pains, and weight gain seen in men from industrialized countries whose wives are pregnant as "couvade syndrome."

What's going on here? The practice of couvade doesn't mean that the pain women in most cultures feel during childbirth isn't "real." Nor does it mean that the men who practice couvade are feeling "fake" pain. Rather, it underscores the importance of the expectations we have for pregnancy and childbirth.

Men have little guidance about what they should do and feel during the preceding nine months. The roles our fathers played during pregnancy and childbirth seem alien and inappropriate. At the same time, the good-natured kidding we receive from friends and coworkers may raise our anxieties about fatherhood.

The physical and the emotional changes women undergo during pregnancy are obvious and serve to underscore their shift into motherhood. For men, the changes are more subtle, and may undermine rather than bolster our confidence as beginning parents.

The confusion an expectant father feels is often made worse when he accompanies his wife to a prenatal examination or some other activity that was previously "for women only." Men are now more readily accepted and even welcomed at prenatal checkups and in the delivery room or, if the woman undergoes a cesarean section, in the operating room. But there is still a feeling that we are trespassing.

[3]R. Melzack, *The Puzzle of Pain* (New York: Basic Books, 1973), p. 22.

Dr. Shapiro recalls being bumped into by three nurses during one prenatal visit. Each bump was followed by the nurse saying, "Excuse me!" with thinly veiled sarcasm and hostility. In an extreme case, one of the men he interviewed for his study was told, "OK, you can be present, but if you faint, don't expect us to worry about you lying on the floor with all the blood and gore. We'll just have to kick you out of the way and go about our business." Another man, who insisted on being at his second child's birth, was strapped to a wheelchair "for his own protection."

The negative messages fathers receive today are often more subtle, but can be found even in hospitals that say they welcome their involvement. After the birth of my own son, I recall several hospital staff members who would talk to my wife about caring for our child without ever looking at me, even though I was only a few feet away. It was a clear message that I was an intruder or perhaps even irrelevant to these woman-to-woman talks about caring for our baby.

But not all men want to be actively involved in childbirth. Sometimes pregnant women are confused and angered by their husband's flat-out refusal to be present during labor and delivery. Whenever I've seen this, the cause has usually been the same: fear of shaming himself.

The mental images these men have of childbirth are distorted and terrifying. They worry that they will faint or vomit at a critical moment, and have to live down that episode for the rest of their lives. (Being men, they won't tell you this directly, of course. They'll usually mutter something about how their mothers made it through labor alone or say that you will be embarrassed to have them around.)

Rather than look for ways of handling their fears, such as learning more about what will take place during labor and delivery, they dodge and deny their emotions. If you try to argue the logic of the situation with your husband, it won't work. He's not thinking logically, although he'll strongly tell you he is. Instead, address the emotions lurking below the surface. Suggest that you attend childbirth classes together and watch some videotaped births. If he's reluctant to do that, encourage him to talk to other men who've attended childbirth classes or to talk to the instructor. If that doesn't work, then you should talk to the instructor about your situation—and perhaps find an alternate labor coach.

During his study of several hundred expectant fathers during the 1980s, Dr. Shapiro found that *more than half* acknowledged having at least fleeting thoughts or fears that they were not the biological father of the child. Yet when he asked the fathers whether they thought their wives had been unfaithful, many felt insulted by the question. It's a fascinating paradox, which shows us the ambivalence with which many men approach pregnancy. Questioning paternity may be a way for the man to deny the changes he is facing in his life and to distance himself from the pregnancy. Most of these men kept their concerns to themselves. Their spouses were unaware of their husbands' feelings.

Men are more likely than women to express their emotions through actions rather than words. Instead of talking about his concerns over being able to care for his expanding family, a man will often behave in ways that address those concerns symbolically. He may take on additional work during the pregnancy as a way of coping with the fear that he will not be able to provide enough financial support. He may visit old friends he's neglected to reassure himself that he won't have to give up his social life.

A psychiatrist I interviewed told me of a writer he knew who had taken on an extra assignment when he learned that his wife was pregnant. When her labor contractions were close together, she told him she wanted to go to the hospital. He replied that he wanted to finish one last paragraph. It was as if he needed to finish his own creative work before she could do hers.

◆   ◆   ◆

SPECIAL TASKS FOR MEN
DURING PREGNANCY

The physical changes of pregnancy constantly remind women of how their lives will change as well. Men may need some extra help coming to terms with their new roles as fathers and their changing relationships as spouses. Here are some things men (and couples) can do to help prepare themselves emotionally for the first stage of parenthood:

◆ Schedule some discussions with your spouse about your feelings on being a parent. Don't talk about just your emotions, but also some nitty gritty details, like who's going to get up at three A.M. when the baby is crying, and who will change the first diaper of the morning.

Ideally you should have these discussions both before the pregnancy and during its first few months. Keep in mind that your goal is not to set schedules or negotiate contracts, but to let each other know what you are thinking, and to begin focusing on the changes in your day-to-day lives. If you have different assumptions and expectations, it's better to discover them now than when the baby is screaming in the wee hours of the morning.

◆ Go to prenatal checkups together. Some men feel uncomfortable about office visits, because they don't know where they should stand. They may also be unsure of what they should do (and how they should feel) during the examination. It's a good idea to discuss these issues ahead of time.

One of the climactic moments of an early prenatal checkup is being able to listen to the baby's heartbeat. This is especially important for men, since it's often the first concrete evidence they have that their baby is alive.

◆ Attend childbirth classes as a couple so you know what to expect during a normal labor and delivery. For many men, these classes serve as a necessary confirmation that the pregnancy is real, and that it's only a temporary condition.

Studies by Dr. Philip A. Cowan at the University of California at Berkeley have shown that men are often several months behind women in acknowledging and accepting the changes they face as parents. Wives who expect their husbands to be at the same stage of acceptance and excitement are often disappointed by their husbands' words and behaviors. Men who attend childbirth classes, go to prenatal examinations, feel their baby kicking, and otherwise become active participants in the pregnancy tend to be more advanced and realistic in their understanding of what's happening and what's in store for them.

♦ Share your feelings and fears with your spouse or partner and with other men. Many men who were interviewed for studies of how prospective parents respond to a pregnancy said they felt that their positive feelings about the pregnancy were welcome, but that their fears and anxieties were not.

Many men feel sad during a pregnancy. The emotion often surprises them. Even though a man may have wanted to become a parent, he now recognizes that he may lose some of his wife's love. The unborn baby has become a rival.

Men may also feel that the baby is robbing them of their youth. For many men, caring for a baby is a completely new and even frightening type of responsibility. They have never had someone who was so totally dependent on them. Beneath their veneer of confidence or their active avoidance of the topic, they may worry that they are not up to the task. It's important to address these issues, even if they're unspoken.

♦ Talk to your baby before he or she is born. You can even try singing to your baby. That's one of the simplest ways to help you realize, at an emotional level, that you're already interacting with a real person.

♦   ♦   ♦

The Emotions of Pregnancy and Childbirth

I feel like a time bomb ready to explode!
—A WOMAN I INTERVIEWED, WHO WAS PREGNANT
WITH TRIPLETS

We've seen how the parent-child relationship begins long before we give birth to our children. We form bonds in our mind when we decide to have a child, realize we are pregnant, or choose to adopt. The images we carry with us while we wait to meet our newborn children influence not only how we feel about them, but also about our spouses and ourselves.

That's why it's so important to know what to expect emotionally during a pregnancy. (Adoptive parents will find that many of the same things happen to them, even though they're not biologically pregnant.) If you can anticipate the rocky and stressful passages, they are less upsetting and less likely to cause damage to your relationship with your spouse.

To many first-time parents, pregnancy marks an emotional transition: from woman to mother, from man to father. For some it is an even bigger jump from boy or girl to adult. You begin to view yourselves in a new light. Suddenly you are on par with your own parents, who seemed so knowledgeable (and so old!) when you were a young child.

You may find that your parents, other relatives, and even friends treat you differently. Pregnant women often notice that they feel closer to their mothers than they have in years. This is especially true toward the end of the first trimester and the beginning of the second. Expectant mothers' thoughts turn inward as they come to terms with their new roles and relationships. It is a time when pregnant women often report a significant increase in the time they spend talking on the telephone with and visiting their own mothers. They are, perhaps, looking for a key to understanding what is happening to them, to help them interpret those important changes.

Men sometimes respond to this by feeling neglected and jealous. They don't understand why their wives are so obsessed with their pregnancies and spend so much time sharing their emotions with others. They may become resentful of their mothers-in-law, and incorrectly blame them for their wives' emotional changes.

At the same time, men often find themselves renewing old contacts outside the family, such as long-neglected friends. Psychologists usually interpret this as a search for reassurance that not everything will change with the arrival of the child. "Deep down inside, I'm still the same old me!"

OLD RULES, NEW GUILT, AND THE "PREGNANCY POLICE"

The onset of pregnancy brings with it a host of concerns. We worry about competence. Are we up to the tasks ahead? Can we care for our growing family? We worry about safety. Will our child be healthy? Will we be healthy? (When my wife became pregnant I switched from drinking whole milk to low-fat milk—something I had put off for years. Looking back on it, it seems so wonderfully symbolic. Was this, perhaps, my way of contributing to my new son's nutrition by giving up something of my own?)

At its extreme, which is unfortunately all too common, prospective parents fear that anything they do "wrong" will automatically lead to a lifelong problem for their child. There's a clear relationship between having a low-birthweight, high-risk baby and not getting good prenatal care, or abusing your body by taking alcohol and certain drugs. But that doesn't mean that your child will suffer fetal alcohol syndrome if you had one drink before you realized you were pregnant.

It's a matter of playing the odds. Clearly, your baby is safer if you don't drink, smoke, or use street drugs (and certain prescription drugs as well) while you're pregnant. If you want the odds on your side, you should avoid those things and eat healthily as soon as you decide to get pregnant.[1]

But the statistical probabilities associated with many of these guidelines for pregnancy are often ignored in favor of simple and sometimes questionable rules. ("Gain at least twenty-four pounds." "Eat five hundred calories per day over your normal diet." "Don't eat any chocolate when you drink milk because it decreases your body's ability to absorb cal-

---

[1]To give you some perspective on the odds of having a healthy baby in the United States, and what you can do to increase those odds, here are some of the most recent figures from the National Center for Health Statistics. Although they don't record whether a baby is "healthy," birth certificates do list a child's birth weight. Since a low birth weight (less than twenty-five hundred grams or five pounds eight ounces) is highly associated with health problems, it serves as a pretty good measure of how well a newborn is doing. In fact, low birth weight is the single most important predictor of infant death.

According to figures from 1989 published in the April 15, 1992, issue of *Monthly Vital Statistics Report* (Vol. 40, No. 12, Supplement), 7.2 percent of children were born with a low birth weight. That's roughly one in fifteen babies.

Among smokers, however, 11.4 percent of their babies (more than one in nine) were of low birth weight, compared with 6.0 percent of nonsmokers. So smoking *doubles* your chances of having an underweight baby.

cium.") These days such rules are often enforced by self-appointed "pregnancy police" who rush in to tell you how everything you're doing will cause problems. Unfortunately, what these people lack in knowledge or perspective they make up for in enthusiasm.

It's easy to get swept up in these rules, and to feel both overwhelmed and terribly guilty. Will that one glass of wine or the single cigarette you had during pregnancy lead to brain damage? Will your child be hyperactive because you didn't eat the right vegetables or craved salty snacks during your first trimester?

Too many books on pregnancy provide readers with a list of things they should and shouldn't do. By listing them equally, they imply that each item is equally important. Since everyone does something on the "no-no" list and doesn't do at least one thing from the "must do" list, I worry that these simple-minded prescriptions encourage mothers to give up on some important healthy behaviors, since they're told they've already failed. What a terrible way to begin motherhood!

Keep in mind that fetuses are remarkably resilient. Breaking an occasional minor "rule" probably won't make any difference. (Ignoring a major commonsense guideline, like not seeking adequate prenatal care, smoking a pack of cigarettes a day, or getting drunk, is much more likely to lead to serious problems, however.) If you're worried about the effect of that chocolate bar you had with your milk earlier, just drink another glass of milk now. Life's too short to give up chocolate.

◆　　◆　　◆

ATTITUDE AND INFORMATION

I recently received a book in the mail that was aimed at pregnant women. It was, in essence, a three-hundred-page checklist of things to worry about. The book was so scary that, if you read it before getting pregnant, you might very well decide not to have children.

While I'm a firm believer that you should get all the information you need to feel comfortable, this sort of detailed questionnaire verged on the paranoid. (I especially liked the part that asked if you were planning to store hazardous chemicals near your baby's crib! Needless to say, the authors implied this was a bad idea.)

For many expectant parents, what helps them handle their anxieties even more than information is an attitude about obtaining that information. When it comes to health care, all too often we abdicate our rights to question and understand what's happening to us. We stop being people and start being patients. We forget that, although it's their hospital or clinic, it's *our* body and *our* baby!

In many ways, this attitude is a return to childhood, where we learned that asking a question may be perceived as a sign of stupidity. In fact, the truth is the opposite. It's also a reflection of the imbalance of power that pervades hospitals and clinics. It's easy to come away feeling that your health-care needs are little more than an imposition on the time of the professional staff instead of their reason for being there.

Often these messages are subtle. When I worked at the Mayo Clinic, the dress code stated that I was expected to wear a suit. Few of the parents I spoke with dressed that formally. I sensed that the difference in our "uniforms" acted as a barrier to open communication. To break through that barrier, I would go through a ritual of taking off my jacket and loosening my tie as soon as I walked someone to my office. This gave them the impression that I wasn't rushed and would take whatever time was needed to listen to their questions and concerns. As soon as they left, I'd tighten my tie and put on my jacket so that I could go through the same routine with the next person I saw.

Here are some ways to help yourself get the information you want about your pregnancy and your baby:

♦ Use a notebook. It's a good idea to write down questions as they occur to you, even if it's a few weeks before one of your prenatal checkups. That way you won't forget to ask them when you have the opportunity. You should also use the notebook to write down the answers. This actually serves two purposes: It ensures that you won't forget what you've learned, and it forces the person giving you the information to slow down while talking to you.

♦ Ask how unfamiliar words are spelled. Write them down in your notebook. That way, you can always look up more information later.

♦ Don't assume you have to get all the information you want from your physician. Many people feel less pressured when they talk to a nurse practitioner, nurse midwife, health educator, or childbirth educator.

♦ If you're feeling brushed off or ignored, point it out tactfully. Sometimes health professionals aren't aware of how they're coming across, especially at the end of a busy day. If that doesn't work, ask to speak to someone else who might be able to address your concerns.

♦ Remember that asking questions is a sign of intelligence and competence. No one was born knowing what you want to find out.

♦   ♦   ♦

DREAMS OF A LATER RELATIONSHIP

Many parents describe pregnancy as a time of intense dreaming—both literally and figuratively. During the daytime, we may imagine our children at play or at school. We fantasize about what they will be like as adults. Will they become famous movie stars or win a Nobel prize? Will they be the first in the family to go to law school or to live in Paris or Beijing? Will they be so financially successful that they'll send us on a cruise around the world? (Little Jennifer and José aren't even born, and we're already putting pressure on them!)

But at night, prospective parents often have other dreams that may be unsettling or even frightening. Although these dreams may give us clues to what's bothering us at a subconscious level, it's important not to interpret them literally. They are *not* omens or predictions of things to come. Through our dreams we can purge ourselves of our deepest fears. We can also sometimes use dreams to see our problems from a new perspective and, perhaps, gain insight into how to solve them.

Many prospective parents report having (or at least remembering) more nightmares than usual. Some of these directly involve their unborn child. You may dream that he is deformed or otherwise damaged. You may dream that, after he is born, you have misplaced him or forgotten to feed him. You may have dreams in which you are terribly angry at your baby.

In each case, the dream is a reflection of your unconscious thoughts and feelings toward becoming a parent. The hostility toward your baby expressed in a dream is usually a reflection of the normal but hidden feelings parents have toward the fetus. We keep these feelings to ourselves—often hiding them from ourselves, in fact—because they are not socially accepted.

Pregnancy is a time when parents feel they have less control over their lives than usual. They are searching for ways to regain that feeling of predictability. This makes pregnant couples more likely to become superstitious. Unfortunately, those superstitions are often accompanied by unnecessary worries and feelings of guilt.

Pregnant women resent, at times, the changes that their bodies are undergoing. This is especially true in a culture like ours which puts a high value on thinness, agility, and stamina—all of which disappear or diminish during pregnancy. This resentment turns to anger toward the two people around the pregnant woman: her spouse and her unborn child. While the anger toward her spouse can be expressed while she's awake, the feelings of resentment toward her unborn child are more commonly expressed through dreams.

Men may have similar dreams, which they may find especially disturbing. Pregnancy often makes a man feel like a rival with his unborn child for his spouse's attention and affection. Like a preschooler trying to cope with the birth of a new sibling, the prospective father may dream of disposing of the child so that he may regain his rightful place. He may also feel conflicts between his wife's sexuality or sexual attractiveness and her new role as a mother.

It's important to remember that these feelings are normal. They're not a sign that you're a bad parent or that there is anything wrong with your child. Rather, they show the seriousness with which you are taking the responsibilities of parenthood. Think of them as cues for discussion between the two of you or, if you're a single mother, a discussion with your own mother or another experienced parent.

◆   ◆   ◆

INTERPRETING YOUR DREAMS

A psychology professor of mine developed a strong interest in dreams and their interpretation. To help him understand and remember his own dreams, he spent several weeks with a tape recorder by his bed. Whenever he woke up in the middle of the night after a dream, he would record as much as he could remember. That way he wouldn't forget the details by morning.

One morning he recalled having awakened from a particularly vivid dream several hours earlier. Although he couldn't remember the content of the dream, he distinctly recalled thinking, "I've got to get this down on tape!" When he looked at the tape recorder, he saw that he'd recorded something that night.

Flushed with excitement, he rewound the tape and started to play it back. On the recording, he heard himself saying over and over, "I've got to get this down on tape! I've got to get this down on tape!" It was the only thing he had recorded.

Dream interpretation is a complex subject filled with everything from obscure symbolism to gross oversimplifications. The instructions in this box aren't intended to teach you how to analyze your dreams. Instead, I hope they'll serve as a structure that will help you discuss your dreams about parenthood and the feelings behind them with your spouse or someone else you trust.

Begin by writing down answers to the following questions. Remember, you only have to write a few words in response to each question.

♦ In one sentence, what was the plot of your dream?

♦ How did you feel during the dream? (Excited? Fearful? Detached?)

♦ How did you feel as soon as you woke up? (Frightened? Pleased?)

♦ What details in the dream surprised you? (Something about yourself? Something about your child?)

♦ Have you had this dream or a similar dream before? If so, when? (Before some big event, like getting married or starting a new job? When you were a child?)

♦ How worried or upset are you by this dream?

♦ What aspect of the dream is bothering you? (The plot? The emotions? The people? The images?)

♦ How realistic do you think the dream is? Why? (Are you worried that it foretells the future? Is it a reflection of your own childhood?)

♦ What do you think the dream is saying to you symbolically? Why? (Will you be a successful parent? Will you fail? Should you be doing something differently?)

♦ How do you think your spouse or some other important person would react to your having this dream? Why? (Anger? Fear? Closeness?)

After you've written down a few words in response to each of these questions, share your dream and your reactions to it with your partner. Don't try to interpret the subtle details, like whether the baby was in a carriage or a crib. Instead, focus on the emotions. By doing this, you'll often find yourselves talking about some aspects of your relationship or of parenthood that you've never discussed before.

◆　◆　◆

RAGING HORMONES, CHANGING EMOTIONS

You don't need to look at dreams to see the mental stresses that accompany pregnancy. Given the number of emotional, physical, and relationship changes people are undergoing, it's surprising to see so many parents who stay reasonably stable.

Some of the emotional changes and mood swings we associate with pregnancy have obvious causes. (It's difficult to be cheerful at the beginning of the day when you know you'll be facing morning sickness.) Others are more symbolic and may be easily missed or misinterpreted. As with dreams, sharing your feelings with your spouse often helps both of you gain a new and better perspective.

There appears to be a biological trigger for some of the quick and dramatic changes in moods many pregnant women undergo. The large releases of hormones and other biological changes, as well as the growing awareness of the long-term implications of having a child, are often reflected in pregnant women's emotional lability. You may be surprised to find yourself crying over movies that, six months earlier, you would have described as melodramatic or even silly. You may have uncharacteristic flashes of anger which are quickly followed by feelings of deep remorse.

This emotional lability is especially disturbing to women and couples who pride themselves on their rational, reasonable natures. All of a sudden a woman who spends her days as a tough-minded corporate attorney or highly organized retail manager starts crying uncontrollably when she hears a particular song on the radio—and she doesn't even like the song! Getting upset with herself, or hearing her spouse getting angry at her, makes things even worse.

I often tell pregnant couples that one of the best gifts they can give each other at this time is increased tolerance and forgiveness. Expect a little craziness and more than a little frustration to accompany the pregnancy. Forgetfulness, for example, is a common side effect of pregnancy, especially in the final months. While it sometimes happens in men as well, it's more common among women. Don't interpret it as a sign that you are losing (or have already lost) your sanity. While some of it may have to do with the biochemical changes in your pregnant body, it's most likely a reflection of the intensity with which you've been focusing on the pregnancy. If you want, simply carry a small notepad with you. (Of course, you may forget the notepad.)

Forgetfulness can be tremendously frustrating for both parties. If a pregnant woman becomes absentminded, she may worry that she'll be unfit as a mother. Her husband, who's also feeling under stress, may interpret her forgetting something as a way of intentionally annoying him. A forgotten shopping list or library book can quickly trigger a major argument.

That's where the gift of tolerance and forgiveness comes in. It's helpful to tell yourself and your partner that it's only a passing stage. Things will get better as soon as the baby is born and you've had a chance to catch up on your sleep—which any parent will tell you takes about four years.

SHARING THE EMOTIONS OF PREGNANCY

Although our culture generally categorizes pregnancy as a joyful event, many prospective parents are surprised by the mixed feelings it generates. Becoming pregnant churns up deep and sometimes forgotten memories in both parents. It causes us to reevaluate our roles and our accomplishments. It leads us to face up to our own mortality in a new and profound way.

It's important to talk about the realities of pregnancy with people who have gone through it recently and, if possible, with professionals such as obstetrics nurses and childbirth educators who deal with it daily.

For men, talking to another recent father can help tremendously. So can attending childbirth education classes, which have become more sensitive to the emotional side of pregnancy for both parents. It's always good to know that other people have gone through what you are feeling, and have survived.

Yet talking to other people about our emotions during pregnancy can take some courage and some planning. Think of the number of times during the day that you're asked how you're feeling. Our culture has taught us from the time we are children that such a question is usually perfunctory. It's little more than an acknowledgment of our presence, and should be answered with as short a phrase as possible: "OK." "I'm fine." "Not bad."

Yet pregnancy is a time when both parents are eager to share how they really are feeling. We need to affirm ourselves. We need to find out if others have felt this way. We need to hear a touch of sympathy or a gush of pride.

"How are you feeling today?"
"I feel as if my whole life is changing! It's exhilarating and it's a bit frightening."
"I'm proud of what we've done, but I'm worried about what the future may hold."
"We've wanted this baby for a long time, but I don't know if we're really ready for it."

I'm not saying that you need to overload everyone you meet with your thoughts about what's happening in your life. (That's a sure way to lose your popularity.) But you need to look for times when you can go beyond the superficial day-to-day conversations and search for support from others who have been where you are.

THE EMOTIONS OF CHILDBIRTH

There's a tremendous and fascinating variation in how mothers and fathers react to childbirth. Your emotional response appears to bear little relationship to how long or strenuous labor is. The intensity and scope of your feelings appear to be strongly influenced by such things as what you expect labor to be like, and what its symbolic meaning is to you.

We find these links between emotions, expectations, and symbolism in other areas of medicine as well. When I did research at the Mayo Clinic on psychological factors that influenced recovery from surgery, I was surprised at the wide range of pain people felt when they underwent the same operation.

Earlier researchers had commented on how, during World War II, many soldiers who were seriously but not critically wounded needed little if any morphine. One study of American soldiers wounded at Anzio found that only 32 percent requested narcotics to control their pain. Yet American civilians who had "biologically equivalent" wounds from operations in hospitals had quite a different reaction: 83 percent requested narcotics for pain.

These researchers concluded that a critical variable was the *meaning* of the pain in each case. To the battlefield soldiers, it meant that they were still alive and would probably soon be shipped home. Their lives would improve. To the civilians, it meant that their lives had changed for the worse and that they could look forward to a stressful period of recovery.

To me, this implies that mothers who know the least about what to expect during labor and delivery, who are least prepared for parenthood, and who have the least emotional support from their families and friends will tend to feel more pain during childbirth than mothers who know what to expect, are prepared for parenthood, and feel emotionally supported.

That's one of the reasons why women who attend child-birth education classes report feeling less pain during labor and delivery than women who do not. Some of that comes from what they learn in the classes, such as breathing tech-niques. Some comes from a knowledge of what's happening to their bodies at each stage of the process, and from the active involvement of a partner, most often the father. But some of it is also a matter of self-selection. The people who have the most support from their families and friends are most likely to be able to attend such classes.

I've noticed only one bad side effect of childbirth education, which comes from a distortion of what the educators are trying to share. Some women come away from such programs with the feeling that there is something wrong with them if they request a painkiller during labor. It is as if they have failed as mothers from the very beginning. They feel terribly guilty if their childbirth was not "natural."

Fathers may unconsciously contribute to this, especially since they are not the ones undergoing the physical changes that accompany childbirth. (One woman I know, when asked by a man to describe what childbirth felt like, asked him to imagine grabbing his lower lip and slowly pulling it over his forehead! While her comment was clearly an exaggeration, it made her point.)

It's important to remember that women experience the stress of labor very differently. There's nothing "better" or "stronger" about a woman who reports less pain than an-other or who uses less pain medication. It's a good idea for both parents to talk ahead of time to the physician or midwife who will be with them during the delivery about what their options are regarding pain control. Find out when the various types can be administered, and what temporary effects, if any, they will have on your baby.

Finally, parents should talk to each other about the symbol-ism of using pain medication. Women are not the only ones who worry about whether taking pain medications is a sign of failure. Men, who've been told much of their lives to "tough it out," may view it as a sign of weakness. (These may be the same men, of course, who feel queasy when faced with changing a dirty diaper.) Others may be so emotionally connected to their wives that they may push for medication before the women feel they need it.

Another important thing for prospective parents to prepare themselves for is the loss of control during labor and delivery. Mothers may experience labor as something that is done *to* them. They may resist or go with the flow. Doctors may speed up or slow down the process. But once begun, it is inevitable. It is as if your body has been taken over by a mysterious and powerful force. It may feel like your body is no longer your own.

The hospital apparatus associated with childbirth contributes to these feelings. Although you may have imagined going through the first stages of labor while sitting in a comfortable rocking chair, you may find yourself instead hooked up to a lot of wires and tubes. There may be intravenous lines in your arm and a fetal monitor belt wrapped around your belly.

Some women find the loss of control during labor more upsetting than others. (Nurses on obstetrics units have told me stories of women who, after several hours of difficult labor, ask if they might stop for a while and go home, promising that they'll come back the next day to continue!) Again, childbirth education helps, since it gives both parents a sense of what they can expect.

Undergoing a cesarean section, especially if it was not anticipated and comes after hours of painful labor, can accentuate these feelings of loss of control. Some mothers view it as a failure—that somehow they were not good enough to deliver the "normal" way. Even though they know at an intellectual level that their guilt is misplaced, they feel it nonetheless. Talking ahead of time about the possibility of a cesarean section with each other and with your physician or midwife will help limit those feelings of guilt.

◆   ◆   ◆

THE HOSPITAL BAG

The trip to the hospital at the beginning of labor is a staple for movies and television programs. We've all watched dozens of scenes in which the nervous father grabs (or forgets to grab) that ubiquitous suitcase and dashes off to the hospital, occasionally remembering to bring his wife as well. The scenes are reflections of the times they were shot, when fathers felt they were out of place in a maternity ward, and would not get to see their children until the ordeal was over.

Times have clearly changed. But what about that bag? Its contents have also changed over the past generation to reflect the new expectations for both parents. Some of the contents are obvious, such as a change of clothing for the mother. But there are other, often-omitted things you may wish to pack as well. They can make your life easier while you're at the hospital or birthing center.

One important rule is: Don't bring anything with you that's very expensive or irreplaceable. Jewelry, fancy radios, and the like have an unfortunate tendency to "disappear" during hospital stays. It's not worth the risk. Leave most of your credit cards at home. If you have something especially valuable with you, ask the nurses on your floor if they can store it for you in a locked office.

◆ Labor supplies. Although the hospital will provide you with a gown to wear, there are some other articles of clothes you'll probably want to bring. Pack one or two pairs of warm socks or leggings for when your legs feel cold. Bring a rubber band or headband to keep your hair out of your face—something that can be particularly annoying when you're trying to concentrate on pushing. Take a tube of lip balm for when your lips inevitably feel dry. Pack a bathrobe and slippers, since you're sure to feel more comfortable in your own than in what the hospital will offer you. If you wear contact lenses, remember to pack your alternate glasses as well as the various lens cleaning and storage solutions you use for the contacts.

If you want to take your own pillow, make sure the pillowcase isn't white. That way it won't be mistaken for one owned by the hospital. Pack an inexpensive cassette player and some music you like. (The offerings on radio at three A.M. may not suit your taste.) Bring extra batteries. If you like playing cards or word games, pack some. You may also want to take along some of your favorite short stories or poetry—this isn't a good time to begin a twelve-hundred-page Russian novel.

♦ *Labor-coach supplies.* I always encourage labor coaches to ask the nurses for a scrub suit—the pajama-like outfit worn in operating rooms. They're very comfortable, and you don't have to worry about anything spilling on them. Your kit should include a pair of sneakers or other very comfortable shoes, as well as a change of socks and underwear for your labor coach.

Pack a few nonperishable snacks such as granola bars. It's also a good idea to have enough cash on hand so your coach can order a late-night pizza or other food delivered to the hospital. It may sound silly, but I've found that one of the most predictable reactions coaches have to a prolonged labor is hunger. That's why nurses who work on labor and delivery units are so expert on which pizza delivery services in their area are the best.

♦ *Telephone supplies.* Although you're likely to have a telephone by your bedside, your labor coach may wish to use a pay phone down the hall to tell people about the new baby. This is an especially good idea if it's four A.M. and you've just fallen asleep after thirty-six hours of labor. Besides, you may wish to keep the bedside phone open for incoming calls.

Your bag should include a list of people you want to call, along with their telephone numbers. It's also a good idea to go to the bank and get one or two rolls of coins so that you have enough change with you.

If your friends and relatives are the type who send flowers to congratulate you, encourage them to wait a few days and send them to your home so that you don't

have to worry about taking them home from your hospital room along with your baby. For those flowers that do
arrive at the hospital, rather than carting them home,
consider asking the nurses or volunteer service about
having them delivered to other patients who are staying
longer and could use something to brighten their rooms.

♦ *Supplies for going home.* While the clothing you
wore to the hospital won't fit anymore, neither will what
you wore before you became pregnant. The basic rule
is: Go for comfort, not for fashion. Pack loose-fitting
clothes.

Perhaps the most important thing to remember, even
though it won't fit in your bag, is an infant car seat. Many
hospitals will (rightfully) insist that you have one before
they'll let you take your newborn in a car. (Remember,
your baby should ride backward for the first few months.)
If you don't own one, some hospitals will rent one to
you and show you how to use it.

♦   ♦   ♦

CHAPTER 5

The Competent Newborn

The legs kick and the arms wave. These reflexes increase in
strength, and the impulse patterns of the nerves are gradually
perfected. A thumb for comfort—yes, why not?
The uterus is no silent peaceful environment.
—L. NILSSON, ET AL.[1]

As parents, we are exhausted and emotionally overwhelmed
for the last few weeks of pregnancy and the first few months
after the birth. We may view our newborns mostly in terms
of their insatiable demands for food and diapers. ("I feel like
I'm a vending machine," one breast-feeding mother of a two-
week-old boy told me.) Babies' floppiness and apparent fragil-
ity during their first few weeks of life make us focus on the
things they can't do.

Throughout the nineteenth and the first part of the twentieth century, newborns were regarded by physicians and psychologists as little more than collections of reflexes—as if they
knew nothing, were blind, deaf, and completely incompetent. Babies were thought of as blank slates waiting to be

[1]L. Nilsson, M. Furuhjelm, A. Ingelman-Sundberg, C. Wirsén, *A Child
Is Born* (New York: Dell, 1986), p. 124.

75

written upon by their environments. Parents treated them accordingly. In 1895, a professor of children's diseases, wrote:

> When the baby is just born, it is very little more intelligent than a vegetable. Its soul and its intellect are there, but they are dormant, waiting to be awakened. It has . . . little control over its body, and all its movements are automatic or instinctive. . . . A newborn baby probably cannot see except to distinguish light from darkness, and will not wink when the finger is brought close to its eyes. It seems unable to hear and, at first, cannot smell. It is, in fact, not directly conscious of anything.[2]

Despite overwhelming evidence gathered over the past thirty years that those beliefs are simply not true, popular literature and folktales have perpetuated the myth that a newborn is incompetent. Let me give you an example. I'm a big fan of novels that are medical thrillers. I just finished reading one in which the main character, a pediatrician and genetics researcher, first realizes that his newborn daughter's a genius when, moments after birth, she opens her eyes and looks at him.

> Christ, he thought. *This isn't possible.* A newborn baby can't really see. It can't detect moving objects for several weeks. And it should be several more before it can focus both its eyes.[3]

This, like the earlier quote from the nineteenth-century physician, is total nonsense, of course. But I read and hear myths like this all the time. One possible reason for these strange beliefs is that, until the 1970s, physicians and psychologists often conducted their assessments of newborns with little regard to the baby's level of alertness. Since newborns sleep most of the time, and are drowsy for much of the rest, it isn't surprising that they seemed "out of it." (Try having someone wake *you* up at three in the morning and ask you to do complex math problems in your head—the developmental

[2]Quotation from a Dr. Griffith, cited in S. Quinn, "The Competence of Babies," *Atlantic Monthly*, January 1982, pp. 54–62.
[3]M. Stewart, *Prodigy* (New York: HarperCollins, 1991), p. 7.

equivalent of some of the things we ask newborns to do—and see how well you perform!)

Now that we're more sensitive to infants' mental states, we're noticing new things that they've been able to do all along. There's nothing unusual at all about a newborn who studies you carefully soon after she's born. Most babies will do exactly that, unless the baby absorbed into her own brain too much of an anesthetic or other drug given to her mother during childbirth.

With all this popular misinformation bandied about, it's no wonder that many parents miss some of the marvelous things their new babies *can* do. If you watch closely and know what to look for, babies will show off their skills for you to admire.

LEARNING BEFORE BIRTH

Many of the techniques developed by pediatricians and psychologists to discover what babies know and can do are complex and require a laboratory filled with electronics. Others are remarkably simple and involve little more than patience and awareness. I find those "low-tech" approaches, which any parent can do, a lot more fun. I'll share some of those simpler techniques with you later in this chapter and in the next few chapters as well. But first, let's take a look at what babies can do before they are born.

Ultrasound imaging and some of the new techniques in medical photography have allowed us to see how a human fetus behaves. By the fifth or sixth month of pregnancy, we can watch as the fetus swallows and hiccups, yawns and shows the rapid eye movement we associate with dreaming. Many parents who see ultrasound images of their fetus during the latter stages of pregnancy are surprised to see their child sucking her thumb. If the obstetrician shines a bright lamp on the mother's belly, the fetus will react to the bright spot on the walls of her environment and change position within the womb so she's not bothered by the light's intensity.

All of this takes a lot of coordination. The fetus who sucks her thumb has shown the ability to make purposeful movements and to figure out ways to calm herself down during periods of stress. The fetus who reacts to the light shows the ability to locate objects in space, and to respond to them in a coordinated manner. Perhaps more impressive, however, are the recent discoveries about children's abilities to hear things before they are born and, within limits, to remember after birth the things they have heard.

For all that we think of the unborn child resting and growing in peaceful surroundings, the womb is actually a noisy place with walls that, from the fetus's perspective, constantly shift and rotate as the mother moves and lies down. Adults who talk about "crawling back into the womb" to get some peace and quiet would be severely disappointed by what they find. Dr. Daphne Maurer, a professor of psychology at McMaster University in Toronto who studies newborns, has graphically described what being inside a womb might feel like:

> It can be boomy, bumpy, unsettling and foul tasting. To an adult, withdrawing into the womb would resemble flying cramped inside a light airplane, through turbulent weather, with the taste of air-sickness in your mouth.[4]

Yet the fetus learns to ignore many of these noises and sensations. We can see this learning when we monitor the heart and movement of a fetus who hears a loud sound. The fetus startles at first. Her heart rate goes up and she may move jerkily. If the sound is repeated, the rise in heart rate quickly disappears, and the fetus's spasmodic movements become smoother and, eventually, disappear as well.

Some mothers report that their children are apparently able to remember music that they heard repeatedly before they were born. I recall one mother who said that during her pregnancy, she routinely put up her feet and relaxed in the afternoon as she watched a particular television program. Her

---

[4]D. Maurer and C. Maurer, *The World of the Newborn* (New York: Basic Books, 1988), p. 7.

baby would also quiet down and kick her less often during this daily rest. After the baby was born, the mother noticed that whenever the theme song from that program was played, her baby would become drowsy. Apparently the baby had associated that particular piece of music with his own relaxation!

◆   ◆   ◆

THE MYTH OF THE MADISON AVENUE BABY

Pick up a magazine or newspaper and take a close look at the advertisements for something aimed at the newborn baby or, to be more precise, the parents of that baby. It might be a brand of formula, a crib toy, a disposable diaper, or a diaper service. There's probably a picture of a baby in the advertisement—but the odds are the baby isn't a newborn.

This has nothing to do with the technical or legal aspects of taking pictures of real newborn babies. Photographers do that all the time. Rather, it's a reflection of the mental images we have of our babies before they are born.

It's important when you are pregnant to think about your expectations for your newborn's appearance and behavior. Having realistic expectations will allow you to see some of the wonderful things about your baby that you might otherwise miss. It will also free you from needless guilt if you were to worry about something that's perfectly normal.

We do not accurately imagine what our children will look like as newborns. Unless he was born by cesarean section, it takes a few days or weeks for his pointed head or squashed nose to recover from his grand entrance. He may have fine hair (lanugo) on his shoulders and back. A newborn's head and, if a boy, his genitals, may appear disproportionately large. He may have temporary birthmarks, like "stork bites" (deep-pink patches on the bridge of the nose or elsewhere on the head) or "mongolian spots" (large pigmented patches that look like bruises on the lower back or buttocks).

I've heard surprised adults and older siblings describe their new babies as reminding them of everything from dried fruit ("She looks like a prune!") to space aliens ("Wow, Mommy, he's E.T.!").

There's nothing wrong with any of this. It's all perfectly normal. But the newborn that parents—especially first-time parents—picture in their minds is what Dr. Edward R. Christophersen calls the Madison Avenue baby.[5] This is a baby who, from the moment she is born, smiles, coos, and has the bodily proportions and general appearance of a young toddler.

What they get instead is a *real* baby who spends her day sleeping, crying, eating, dirtying her diapers, and spitting up food. (Have you noticed that we use a lot of euphemisms when we describe newborns' behaviors? Adults vomit, but newborns "spit up." Adults belch, but newborns "bubble." These more delicate terms may help us respond differently toward a baby than we would to an adult stranger who did the same things.)

It's a good idea for both parents—especially first-time fathers who have little experience with newborns—to take a trip to a hospital nursery to see what a one-day-old infant really looks like.

◆   ◆   ◆

TAPPING INTO THE BRAIN
OF A NEWBORN

OK, you've gone through labor. You've delivered your child. Now let's move on to the stuff that's really fun!

Although you were unaware of it at the time, your baby has been getting to know you during the last part of preg-

---

[5] E. R. Christophersen, *Baby Owner's Manual* (Kansas City, MO: Westport Publishers, 1988).

nancy. He's also been developing some preferences that may surprise you.

Put yourself in the position of a researcher for a moment. You want to find out if a newborn can recognize his mother's voice, even though he's only heard it in the womb. The problem is that newborns can't simply tell you that they recognize something. They can't fill out a questionnaire or push a button when they hear something they've heard before. The next question becomes, "What can a newborn do that will tell us if someone or something sounds familiar?"

Some very creative researchers answered this question by noticing the obvious: Newborn babies are very good at sucking on a nipple. So they wired up a nipple to two tape recordings: one of the baby's mother reading a story, and the other of another woman reading the same story. (There are marvelous photographs of newborns hooked up to this apparatus, with cushioned headphones on their ears and a rubber nipple in their mouth. They look for all the world like World War II bomber pilots on a mission.)

By varying the rate of sucking on the nipple, a newborn could choose which voice to hear. When tested this way, they almost always choose their mothers' voices. This is particularly impressive when you consider that the voices they heard in the womb were distorted and muffled.

Also, newborns offered the same method of choosing what to listen to and given a choice between hearing their mothers read the story that had repeatedly been read aloud during the last few weeks of pregnancy, and one that was new, consistently preferred to hear the one that was read during the pregnancy.

But you don't need fancy laboratory equipment to show this. If a newborn is placed between two women, each of whom talks softly to him, he will almost always turn his head to the sound of his mother's voice. (If the choice is between two strangers, the child will generally turn to the woman whose voice is softer and higher-pitched.)

If the father's been around and talking to the baby during the latter stages of pregnancy, the newborn will, most of the time, turn toward his voice instead of another man's. This isn't as common, however, as choosing the mother's voice.

One pediatrician I know uses this demonstration to help hesitant fathers of newborns feel emotionally connected to their children immediately after birth. He holds the baby at arm's length, and invites the father to talk to his child from one side while he, the doctor, does the same thing from the other. Roughly four out of five babies, he claims, will spontaneously turn toward the father—often leading Dad to spontaneously cry out in delight, "She knows me!"

Suddenly, the father sees his newborn child in a totally different light. A special connection between them is made. They begin to bond. (My pediatrician friend admits that for the one-in-five babies who don't, he subtly and gently rotates their heads so that it looks like they recognize their fathers, who respond with predictable joy and never notice the sleight of hand.)

◆   ◆   ◆

A DIFFERENT "NO MORE TEARS" FORMULA

I'd always heard from parents and nurses that most newborn babies hate having their hair washed. The temperature of the water or the gentleness of the person doing the washing doesn't seem to matter. That comment intrigued me. Not being one to back off from a challenge, I decided that when my son was born, I would get him to like having his scalp shampooed.

The reason I thought I could get him to do it was that I knew how competent newborn babies are. They can learn to associate an experience, such as a flash of light or having their head rubbed, with an emotion, such as fear or happiness.

For the first two days, every time he was breast-fed or bottle-fed and I was around, I would gently stroke his head in small circles. My goal was to have him associate having his scalp rubbed with the feelings of pleasure and satisfaction he got from eating.

I felt a bit awkward doing this—like a mad scientist in a grade-B movie who can't wait to experiment on his own child! Even though I couldn't imagine anything bad coming from it, I didn't tell my wife or the nurses what I was doing.

At the end of the second day the nurse came into our room and announced that she was going to show us how to wash our baby's hair. She warned us that he was very likely to cry and scream, but that we should know this was normal. I told her that I knew our son wouldn't cry.

I'm sure she attributed my comment to a combination of misplaced parental pride and wishful thinking.

She carried him to the sink and gently began to rub his scalp with water and shampoo. She braced for the inevitable yell. Instead, a smile and a look of total satisfaction came over his face. He had learned, during his first two days of life outside the womb, to associate having his head rubbed with feelings of pleasure.

◆   ◆   ◆

CHAPTER 6

Early Learning

For years, scientists thought the reason newborn babies waved their eyes around in such seemingly random ways was that they couldn't really focus on anything, but we now know that, thanks to the fact that they have such small eyes, they can actually see molecules whooshing around, which is a much more interesting thing to watch than a bunch of parents and relatives waving stupid rattles in their faces.

—DAVE BARRY[1]

A FIRST TASTE OF THE OUTSIDE WORLD

If he's not feeling overwhelmed by any medications you received during labor and delivery, your baby will appear to be much more alert during the first twenty-four hours of life than he will during any day over the next few months. He is surrounded by new sensations: movement and abrasion, cold and dryness, clear light and high-pitched sounds.

As if the algebra exams and spelling bees he'll have to face in school aren't enough, your baby will be quickly tested to see how well he's handling his new environment. The most likely first test is known as the Apgar, which is given one minute and five minutes after birth.

The name serves to tell you which physician developed the

[1]D. Barry, *Babies & Other Hazards of Sex* (Emmaus, PA: Rodale Press, 1984), p. 42.

test (Dr. Virginia Apgar) and also, through some tortured English involving the *g*, is a mnemonic for the five items that are evaluated or tested: Activity, Pulse, Grimace (or reflex irritability—a measure of responsiveness), Appearance, and Respirations.

This isn't as esoteric as it sounds. If you watch the nurse or midwife test your baby, you'll get a good general idea of how well he's handling the transition to the outside world.

Although babies don't show test anxiety regarding the Apgar, I've known many parents who do. It's important to keep in mind that babies who score between seven and ten points are doing very well. A baby who scores a ten isn't necessarily any healthier (or smarter or more emotionally stable) than one who scores a seven. A score from four to six is a reason for the physician to be mildly concerned, especially if that score doesn't improve on the five-minute Apgar. (As my high school guidance counselor used to say about how college admissions offices look at report cards, the trend is as important as the actual grades.)

So let's take a minute to look at what's involved in the Apgar test. Babies are awarded zero, one or two points in each category as follows:

Item	0 Points	1 Point	2 Points
Activity	Limp	Some arm and leg movement	Active motion
Pulse (beats/minute)	Absent	Less than 100	More than 100
Grimace[2]	No response	Grimace	Cry, cough, or sneeze

[2]This is usually tested by placing something mildly annoying, like the tip of a bulb syringe or a catheter, just inside the baby's nostril and watching the irritation on his face as he reacts to it.

(continued)

Appearance (color)	Body blue or pale	Hands and feet blue	Healthy color all over
Respirations	Absent	Slow and irregular, weak cry	Good strong cry

Over the next day or so, your child may be given some other tests, such as the Dubowitz (which tests neurological reflexes and gives an indication of your child's age since conception) or the Brazelton Neonatal Assessment Scale (which tests, among other things, whether your newborn will turn her head to follow a moving rattle, stay focused on the examiner's face, and is able to be consoled when upset).

You should watch these tests, if you get a chance. Ask your pediatrician to show you some of the reflexes and other responses your baby was born with. Here are some to look for:

The Moro reflex: The easiest way to elicit this dramatic reaction is by holding your baby horizontally on her back and, while still protecting her in your arms, let her "free fall" for a few inches as if she were being dropped. (While physicians do this all the time as a demonstration to medical students, they're usually reluctant to do it for parents who may worry that they'll actually drop the baby.) You can also sometimes elicit the Moro reflex with a loud noise that startles the baby or by simply letting the baby's head drop an inch.

You'll see that she suddenly tenses, arches her back, and throws her head back. At the same time, she'll spread her arms and legs apart with her hands open, and then bring them abruptly back toward her body with her hands closed. The baby will also cry, which may startle her again and lead to more crying.

The Moro reflex usually disappears by the time the baby is three months old. Since we also see this reflex in other primates, one hypothesis is that it's a throwback to a time when a falling baby might need to quickly grasp her mother's fur.

The palmar and plantar grasp: Stroke your baby's palm with your finger. You'll find that he quickly grabs ahold of you. His grip is actually quite strong at this point, often enough that you can lift him up—though keep in mind that you should always support a newborn's head until his neck muscles develop, and that you should support him in some other way in case he hasn't read a book on child development and decides to let go.

You can do the same thing with your baby's foot—except for lifting him up, of course. If you stroke near his toes, your baby will try to grab your finger with them. The palmar grasp—the one with the fingers—usually disappears in about six months. The plantar grasp lasts a few months longer.

This reflex is also seen in other primates. Dr. Richard M. Restak[3] describes how the palmar reflex is used in some Asian countries to capture monkeys. The trappers hollow out a coconut, place some sweet food inside, and hang it beneath a tree branch. At the bottom of the coconut is a slit large enough for a monkey to pass his open hand through, but too small for his fist. The monkey reaches in, touches the food, and reflexively grasps it. But now his closed fist is too big for the slit. He can't open his hand because of the reflex, so he's trapped—a victim of his own nervous system.

The Babinski reflex: As long as you're playing with your baby's feet, try drawing your thumbnail up the sole of his foot. You'll notice that his toes will fan upward and outward. That's an indication of how immature and incomplete your baby's nervous system is. If you were to try this nine months later, his toes would move in the opposite direction—unless he had certain types of brain damage, in which case he'd respond to the stroking like a newborn.

Ask your pediatrician to show you the proper way to test for the Babinski reflex. Once, when I was in college, I was involved in a minor accident at a hospital where I worked. The intern who examined me in the emergency room ran his

[3]R. M. Restak, *The Infant Mind* (Garden City, NY: Doubleday, 1986), pp. 4–5.

thumb up the sole of my foot, and noticed that I fanned my toes like a newborn and reflexively jerked my foot away. He called over the attending neurologist and explained that he wanted to hospitalize me for a brain-damage workup.

The neurologist asked the intern to demonstrate the test again. He did, and once again my toes fanned and I jerked my foot away. The neurologist then patiently explained to the intern that I didn't have to be hospitalized because he already knew the diagnosis: The intern wasn't doing the test correctly, and I was ticklish!

The tonic neck reflex: This is sometimes called the "fencer's reflex." With your baby lying on his back, try turning his head to one side. When you do this, he'll extend his arm on the side that he's facing, flex the opposite arm, and draw his knees up. If you then turn his head to face the other side, he'll reverse his arm positions. With only a little imagination, he looks like a fencer in the *en garde* position.

The walking and swimming reflexes: If you hold your newborn up by his hands so that his feet lightly touch the top of a table—remember, his palmar grasp will make him wrap his hands around your extended finger—he'll move his feet up and down as if he were walking. Some babies will, if you support their weight, actually walk across the table. If you hold him horizontally so that his arms and legs are free, he'll move as if he were swimming.

These are really quite remarkable, and are in some ways different from the other reflexes mentioned earlier. Babies lose these reflexes soon after birth and, must, with a great deal of effort months or years later, relearn at a higher level of their nervous systems the coordinated movements they could do when they were born.

♦   ♦   ♦

AGES, RATIOS, AND PREMATURE BABIES

Unfortunate or not, there is something inherently competitive about being a parent. One of the ways this comes to light is when parents compare how old their children were when they finished a whole bottle, slept through the night, or sat up by themselves. It is a source of pride when our children learn to sit up or recite the alphabet or master toilet training earlier than the other children we know. (The things our friends' and neighbors' children do earlier than ours are all minor or irrelevant, of course!)

But drawing broad conclusions from whether one child passes these developmental milestones, as they are called, earlier or later than another, is fraught with danger and sure to lead to disappointment. I bring this up now because it is a competition that starts during pregnancy and is a particular problem later on for parents whose children are born prematurely.

Most expectant parents find themselves glancing at the many charts in books about child development, wondering if their child will be "on time" or "ahead of schedule" in his development. The mere fact that they're in print and in the form of a table or checklist lends them an undeserved aura of precision. It's that implied precision that gets parents upset if, for example, their six-month-old son can't pick up a small block in his hands because the chart says that's the age at which he "should" be able to do that.

There's one basic rule you should remember about developmental charts that will save you countless hours of worry and heartache in case your newborn baby hasn't been studying them as closely as you have, and decides to follow her own developmental schedule.

That rule is this: *The fact that a child passes through a particular developmental stage is always more important than the age of that child when he or she does it.* In the long run, it really doesn't matter whether you learn to walk at ten months or fifteen months—as long as you learn how to walk. When I lecture around the United States and Canada, I'm often asked questions about toilet training by parents who are obviously upset and worried because their child is "behind schedule." I usually preface my answer by asking how many adults they know who have never been successfully toilet trained!

That's why you really should look at the ages in those charts as an age range instead of a single number. In general, the older the child, the wider the range. after all, children aren't magically able to grasp a small object a certain number of months after being born. It's the culmination of a series of skills involving vision, concentration, muscle coordination, and more. We would naturally expect children to show a significant variation in when they master something that, for them, requires a lot of complicated coordination.

There are two other reasons for this variation or age range. Understanding those reasons takes a bit of arithmetic. This is also where the parents of premature babies can get some much-needed reassurance.

First, when you're trying to figure out roughly when your baby should reach a particular developmental landmark, it's a good idea to start counting from your child's due date instead of the actual day he was born. Remember that being born a month early isn't the same as getting a high school diploma ahead of your peers because you worked extra hard, went to summer school, and skipped a grade.

Physical and mental development takes time. A child who's born two months premature is no more developed than an embryo who will stay in the womb for another eight weeks. The act of being born doesn't speed up that child's growth. Consequently, it's not surprising to find a six-month-old baby who was born two months ahead of schedule to be at the same developmental level as a four-month-old who was carried to term. That's exactly where he should be. But if you simply looked on a chart for six-month-olds, you'd be unnecessarily worried.

Second, look at ratios instead of age differences. This is related to the first point, and explains why we don't worry as much about correcting for a premature baby's age after the first year or two.

The age difference between a six-month-old and a nine-month-old is the same as the difference between a thirty-month-old and a thirty-three-month-old. That's obvious. But the nine-month-old has had 50 percent more time outside the womb to develop, while the thirty-three-month-old has had only 10 percent more time to develop. Consequently, we would expect to see more significant differences in everything from physical coordination to intellectual abilities between the younger children than between the older ones.

That's why we need to recognize that even though the developmental charts are only rough guidelines for the first year, they are even less precise as our children get older. Older children can be years apart in when they reach certain developmental milestones (such as puberty) and still be completely normal.

There's one other important variable that sometimes causes parents needless angst: a false belief in the precision of anything associated with numbers. When I taught a graduate seminar in public health, I would tell my students that my son, according to the medical records from his routine physical examinations, was consistently at about the seventieth percentile for children his age in both his weight and the circumference of his head. The records also showed that he was taller than only about 30 percent of children his age when he was three months old, but bigger than 90 percent of children his age a few months later. I then asked them for the most likely explanation.

I was always amazed at the complexity of their answers, which ranged from rare brain tumors to growth-hormone problems. I then reminded them that babies don't like to lie still and be measured. They squirm. You can get much more reliable measurements of a baby's weight and head circumference because he can move around while you're doing those. The most likely expla-

nation for the difference between the two checkups was
that the nurse wasn't able to get an accurate measure-
ment of his height either time.

In other words, if your data are no good, your conclusion won't be any good either. Or, as computer program-
mers put it: garbage in, garbage out.

◆   ◆   ◆

GAMES THAT SHOW WHAT YOUR
BABY CAN DO

There are some other things you and your baby can try
together from the very first day that will give you a good idea
of how competent she really is and will show you some of
the wonderful things she can do. Begin by testing your baby's
hearing. Hold your baby in front of you, with her feet to your
left and her head supported by your right hand, and gently
say her name. Pay attention to her muscles and what she
looks like. If she gets tense or arches her back, it probably
means she's feeling overwhelmed by what's going on. You
can safely reach the same conclusion if her skin color changes,
her lips start looking a bit blue, or she suddenly spits up.

If she's feeling overwhelmed, try to decrease the stimuli
that are bothering her. Dim the lights in the room. Shut off
radios, televisions, and other sources of unnecessary noise.
Lower your voice to a whisper, and once again, say her
name over and over. She'll probably turn her head in your
direction.

If you pay close attention to how she turns her head, you'll
notice that it's different from the way you and I try to locate
the source of a sound. That's because her head turn is a reflex,
similar to the way she'll turn her head if you gently stroke
her cheek (the rooting reflex.) We know that turning toward
the source of a sound is not just a way of seeing where it's

coming from, because babies will do exactly the same thing in a room that's pitch black when their eyes are closed.

Usually it will take a few seconds for your baby to begin to respond. When she does, she'll move her head very slowly. Dr. Daphne Maurer has labeled this type of response the Jack Benny reflex[4] because it looks like the famous way that comedian did a "take."

Once you've done this with your baby's head in your right hand, you can check her hearing in her other ear by holding her with her head in your left hand. Don't worry if your baby doesn't do this the first time. Feel free to ask your spouse or one of the nurses for some help with the logistics.

You can also get an idea of how well your baby's vision is working by holding her securely in front of you with her head gently supported by your hand. Her face should be a foot away from yours. Odds are her eyes will be moving around, taking in everything in the room. When she glances at you, begin talking to her.

Talk very quietly so that you don't overwhelm her. Say her name. Tell her how smart and pretty she is. Impress her with the fact that her brain will double in size over the next year, and will double once again by the time she's six.

If you pay close attention, you'll probably notice that your voice becomes more high-pitched than normal, even if you don't consciously change it. As you're talking, watch her eyes. Does she stop looking around and begin to focus on your face? (If she doesn't focus on your face the first few times you try this, don't worry. She may not have been looking at you when you started, or she may be too tired. Just try it again later on in the day.)

Keeping her body still, slowly move your face to her left while you quietly talk to her. She'll follow you with her eyes and, perhaps, try to turn her head. Now move your face to her right and see if she still follows you. You can also move

[4]D. Maurer and C. Maurer, *The World of the Newborn* (New York: Basic Books, 1988), p. 136.

up and down relative to your child, or in slow circles around her face to see how well she can track your movement with her eyes. (If it's too awkward to do this with your face, try using a brightly colored rattle.)

Your baby is learning something by looking at you during these first few hours outside the womb. Researchers have found that two-day-old infants look at their mothers' faces longer and differently than they look at the faces of other women. In that brief amount of time, they have learned who you are.

If you'd like some more evidence of how well your baby sees what's going on around her, wait a few weeks and then stick your tongue out at her. I'm perfectly serious. About 50 percent of young babies (a few weeks to a few months old) will mimic the expression on their parents' faces. While she's looking at you, try sticking your tongue in and out a few times. She'll probably start doing the same thing. Try some other facial expressions. Stick out your lower lip as if you were pouting. Open your mouth and eyes as if you were surprised. Smile, and see what happens. In each case, your child will probably change her expression to match yours.

There's another thing you can try after a few days that will help you see how much of a relationship you've developed. Wait until your baby's awake and alert. Start talking to her and watch her eyes focus on your face. Then suddenly stop talking and keep your face frozen. Watch your baby's reaction. She'll probably scan your face with her eyes, looking from your eyes to your mouth and back up again. Then she'll wrinkle her brow and, perhaps, stick out her lower lip. She'll try a variety of things just to get you to respond to her. If you keep your face frozen, she'll probably start to cry.

This tells you how much she's felt a part of your conversation with her, even though she can't understand the words. This is a wonderful demonstration of her special human qualities, even at so young an age. (After all, our pet cats and dogs don't become upset if we try this same experiment with them.) It also shows how important you are in her life.

◆   ◆   ◆

THE ART OF SELF-QUIETING

Another critical but often overlooked skill that babies have is the ability to quiet themselves down when they feel overstimulated. There's tremendous variation in how well individual babies do this when they're born. The ability of their baby to quiet down or comfort herself is very important to parents, for it's the only way they'll be able to get any rest over the next few months. Knowing how skillful your baby is at calming herself will help you recognize when you have to get up to help her at three A.M., and when you can be pretty sure she'll go back to sleep by herself in a few minutes.

You can test her skill at calming herself when your baby's a few days old. Make sure she isn't hungry or cranky or tired, or those problems will make things look worse than they really are. So a good time to try this is soon after you've fed your baby in the morning and she's lying in her bassinet. Jostle the bassinet a little bit so that she starts crying.

Now stop the jostling and look at your watch or a clock with a second hand. Tell yourself that you won't intervene for two minutes. (I tell you to look at a clock because listening to your newborn baby cry for two minutes can feel like two hours!) Pay attention to what your baby is trying to do to relax and regain control of herself. Is she trying to get her fist into her mouth so that she can suck on it? Is she looking at the sides of the bassinet?

If she hasn't calmed down in two minutes, try talking quietly to her. Keep your face about a foot away from hers so that she can focus on it easily. If she's still crying at the end of one minute, try gently holding one or both of her hands to her chest as you talk, or try gently putting one of her hands to her lips to see if she'll suck on it. If she's still crying at the end of a minute of this, try picking her up, holding her close to you, and rocking gently as you quietly say her name.

> Don't be too disappointed if your child needs all of
> this or more to calm down. If you try the same procedure
> in a few weeks, you'll probably notice a significant im-
> provement.

◆   ◆   ◆

MORE GAMES THAT SHOW WHAT
YOUR BABY CAN DO

The more you learn about how much your baby already
knows, and how quickly she's learning new things, the more
impressed you'll be with her development. Perhaps more
important, the more fun you'll have.

Keep in mind that you don't have to spend a lot of money
on fancy toys, and you definitely don't have to build your
own psychology laboratory, to try things that will show off
your child's skills and help you understand how she's thinking. But you do need patience, and a willingness to let your
baby surprise you by not doing the things described in this
or any other book. After all, you wouldn't want your child to
be completely predictable, would you?

Your child's coordination and intellectual capabilities don't
grow at a constant rate. There are fits and starts, plateaus,
and even a bit of backtracking. Don't worry if your baby can
do something one day, but seems to forget it the next.

Also, it's often useful to know what your baby can't do, as
well as what she can do. For example, it takes a few months
for your baby to realize that an object still exists when she
doesn't see it. You and I take that concept for granted. We
know that our beds are still in our bedrooms, even though
we can't see them at the moment. That's simply how the
world works. But young babies don't see the world that way.

If you show a four-month-old baby a shiny set of keys,
she'll probably reach for them. But if she sees you put the
keys behind a cardboard barrier, she won't bother looking for

them. For children this age, it's a case of "out of sight, out of mind." All of this changes when the baby is about ten months old. Suddenly, she'll reach around the cardboard barrier to get the keys, thereby showing you that she understands that they still exist even though she couldn't see them.[5]

All babies like to look at themselves in a mirror, but what do they see? Do they know it's their reflection? Dr. Michael Lewis and Dr. Jeanne Brooks-Gunn, at the University of Medicine and Dentistry of New Jersey and Rutgers University, came up with a fascinating and deceptively simple way of answering that question, which you can try at home.

After letting your child look at herself in the mirror for a minute, briefly pick her up and smear a bit of rouge on her nose or cheek. Most babies under a year old pay little attention to the smudge. A few smile or frown, indicating that they notice something's different.

If your baby seems to notice the rouge, does she reach to touch it? Does she reach for the mirror (an indication that she doesn't think she's looking at a reflection of herself), or does she reach for her own face (an indication that she realizes she's looking at herself)? It's very unusual for a one-year-old baby to see the smudge in the mirror and try to touch it on her own face, yet six months later, about half of them will do so immediately.

But what about things that your baby *can* do? While the experiments that involve sucking on nipples at different rates to trigger specific tape recordings or focus slides are strictly for laboratories, there are other demonstrations you can try that involve only common household objects.

Tie a ribbon or piece of yarn to your baby's ankle or wrist when she's about three months old. Attach the other end to a mobile hanging above her head, or something else that moves or makes a noise she likes. You can even use a helium-

---

[5] Actually, there's some evidence from some studies at the University of Illinois that four-month-old babies may understand the concept of object permanence. But measuring their apparent understanding is much more difficult to do at home.

filled balloon. (One sophisticated version of this demonstration done in Dr. Michael Lewis's laboratory allowed babies to control a picture on a computer screen as well as a recording of a children's song.) Let's say you're letting your baby control the movement of a mobile with her arm.

If you want to act like an experimental psychologist, you can watch your child for a few minutes after you tie the yarn to her, but before you connect it to the mobile. Write down the number of times in each thirty-second period that she moves her arm. Then connect the yarn to the mobile.

At first she'll seem to move her arm randomly. Within a few minutes, she'll notice that the mobile moves when she does. Watch the expression on her face. See if it changes. Write down the number of times she moves her arm every thirty seconds. It will probably go up dramatically. Odds are she's smiling.

After a minute of this, disconnect the yarn from the mobile. Watch her face. She'll probably become frustrated. Her brow will furrow, her eyes will get narrower. She'll pull at the yarn harder or more rapidly. If you reconnect the yarn to the mobile, she'll look happy and excited again.

Although jiggling a mobile sounds trivial, it's a tremendous accomplishment for your baby. She's learned to control her environment. It's a sense of power she obviously relishes, judging by the frustration she showed when the yarn was disconnected.

CHAPTER 7

Adjusting to
Each Other

The demands on me had reached their limit. And I thought, "I
love him, but I would pay all the money in the world to get rid
of him."

—THE MOTHER OF A SEVEN WEEK-OLD BABY

The frustrated and exhausted woman who said that was a
friend of mine from college. She was nurturing, patient, well
educated, loving —and totally overwhelmed. She felt embarrassed by her feelings, as if they meant there was something
wrong with her as a parent.

All parents occasionally have ambivalent feelings toward
their children. We love our kids, but there are times when
we don't really like them, or at least we can't stand what our
children are doing. But most of us keep those feelings to
ourselves, as if it's a dirty little secret. It doesn't fit in with
our images of what we should do and feel as parents.

But it's comforting to know that our first feelings of anger or
resentment toward our children are not only normal, they're
highly predictable. In fact, the timing appears to be linked
directly to the infant's development.

Almost all parents feel negatively toward their babies somewhere in the second or third month of life. Babies tend to cry

more and more every day during the first six weeks.[1] At that age, they're crying about three hours a day, which, considering the number of hours they're sleeping, makes screaming one of their principal activities. (This crying slowly and predictably tapers off; by the time they're three months old, most cry only about one hour per day.)

Meanwhile, as the parent of this infant, you've been trying to cope with new and massive responsibilities under very demanding conditions. You're waking up several times each night to feed, change, and comfort your child, so you're sleep-deprived. You may still feel exhausted from the labor and delivery, or perhaps be recovering from a cesarean section. If it's your first child, you're wistfully recalling the days when you could decide, on the spur of the moment, to go out for dinner or see a movie.

No matter how much support you have, the first few months can be completely overwhelming. The exhaustion can make it even more difficult to learn the skills you need to care for your child. As another friend of mine put it, "I kept wondering when the real mother would show up and take my son away."

Making matters worse, infants don't smile very much until they're about two or three months old. That means you're not getting the social reinforcement that parents of older babies receive from infants who giggle and coo when they're tickled or played with.

Another factor that leads to a lot of anxiety—especially among first-time parents who are past their twenties—is having unrealistic expectations of themselves and their child. Older, inexperienced parents sometimes have idealized images of what raising children will be like. Their bouts of anger and frustration take them completely by surprise.

Feeling that you have to be the perfect parent places a tremendous and completely unnecessary burden on you. If

[1]You can find detailed information about this pattern and how parents respond to it in my earlier book, *Parent & Child: Getting Through to Each Other* (New York: Avon Books, 1992).

we've learned anything from the past half-century's research on child development, it's that children are remarkably resilient. You can make lots of mistakes and still wind up with great kids.

But the pressure to be perfect creates problems of its own. Your expectations of yourself may get in the way of your being a nurturing parent. Your anxieties can be shuttled back and forth between you and your child. A crying baby can cause an anxious parent to become upset. The child senses the parent's discomfort, and cries even more, which increases the parent's frustration.

Parents who fall into this vicious cycle often have difficulty separating their feelings about the child's crying from their feelings about the child as a person. You can become more comfortable and confident as a parent if you realize that there's nothing wrong or unusual about hating your child's behavior, but still loving your child.

◆　　◆　　◆

THE CRY-IT-OUT MYTH

Studies of babies who were raised in institutions such as orphanages found that they cried significantly less at a year old than many babies who were raised by families. The caregivers in the institutions were usually tremendously overworked, so much of the time an upset infant was left alone to "cry it out."

Now, nobody enjoys listening to a crying baby. There appears to be something programmed in our genes that makes an infant's yell much more compelling and motivating than another noise at the same amplitude. As anyone who's ever tried to read peacefully or get some work done on an airplane will tell you, it's extremely difficult not to pay attention to a baby's cry.

There are obvious evolutionary advantages to this. If, thousands of years ago, we had ignored our babies when they were in danger, many more of them would have died, and fewer of us would be around today. But these days, babies are seldom in any real danger when they cry. They may be upset or hungry or cold or lonely, but none of those situations will kill them. So that raises the question, when your baby is crying, why respond at all? Why not let her cry it out? After all, the studies of institutionalized babies showed that they apparently learned to cope with stress without crying.

But when you look closely at the data from those studies of institutionalized babies, something else seems to be going on. They show that, even if you're not concerned with the moral issue of ignoring a crying baby, your best response is to pay attention to the infant who's upset.

By the end of their first year, babies who were *regularly and predictably* comforted when they cried actually cried less than those babies who were raised in institutions and ignored when they cried. The babies who cried the most were those whose parents responded to their cries some of the time, and ignored them some of the time.

Think about this the next time you watch people playing slot machines at Las Vegas or Atlantic City. Every so often their behavior (putting money into the machine) pays off, so they keep doing it. If they get their needs met quickly (they hit the jackpot), they'd probably stop playing for a while. If they never seem to get their needs met (they don't get any money back), they also stop playing and try something else or become depressed. (I'd bet that if you measured the force with which a losing slot machine player pulls the handle, you'd find that he pulls it harder when he hasn't won for a while. It's the equivalent of a baby starting off by crying softly, and then rapidly building the volume to a bellow when no one comes in to comfort him.)

But if their behavior works every so often—that is, sometimes they win a little even if most of the time they lose—they'll keep playing until they're financially or physically exhausted. Psychologists refer to this as a variable ratio reinforcement schedule—you get the response you want on an average of, say, one out of every six tries.

So the best way to decrease the amount your baby cries is to respond quickly to those cries. Sometimes all the child needs is a few gentle words or a bottle. If the crying continues, you can expand your repertoire of baby-comforting techniques: holding, rocking, singing. Like some parents, you may find that marching vigorously around the room with your child in your arms will sometimes do the trick when all else fails.

But keep in mind that there are times when your baby will refuse to be comforted. Try not to take it personally, especially in the beginning when it's so easy to feel as if your child has judged you as a parent and found you lacking. This happens with all babies. It's a part of normal development. But if it happens a lot and you're concerned that something may be wrong, talk to your child's pediatrician.

◆   ◆   ◆

PREMATURE AND "FRAGILE" BABIES

While there are many hospital programs to help the parents of critically ill babies, we tend to pay less attention to those parents whose emotional needs are less obvious. Having a healthy premature baby, or a baby born with a serious but not life-threatening problem like asthma or diabetes, can profoundly color the parent-child relationship.

In these families, the normal adventures of infancy, like leaving the hospital or staying with a baby-sitter for the first time, can stir up strong and unwarranted feelings of concern. All too often, parents think of these babies in terms of their disease or early birth. I've stopped counting the times parents of adolescents have prefaced their descriptions of their children with, "Well, he was premature, you know," as if that somehow explained the children's current difficulties. (It does, however, tell me some things about those parents and what they expect from their children.)

We are right to pay special attention to these children, of course. We should help them get the medical treatment they need and, at times, be more vigilant than usual. But difficulties can occur when you view your children as physically or emotionally fragile even after a medical problem is under control or no longer a concern. Being too protective can sometimes do more harm than the disease.

Inappropriate worries are usually a reflection of the parents' emotions, rather than the child's health. Many parents feel terribly guilty over their child's illness or prematurity, even when it's in no way their fault. You become overprotective, and develop myths about the illness. You may ascribe totally unrelated problems or even the signs of normal development to the illness, which makes you feel even more guilty and protective.

An innovative program at Boston Children's Hospital is trying to break this cycle which, if continued, encourages competent children to feel helpless and not in control. Staff members at the hospital begin by showing the parents of fragile newborns new and more accurate ways of interpreting their babies' behaviors. That way, the parents have the tools and knowledge to focus on their children's strengths, instead of their weaknesses.

For example, a premature infant whose mother is talking to her may feel overstimulated and turn her head away. That's a sign of competency. The child is trying to regulate her environment so that she's more comfortable. But an overprotective mother might interpret the turning away as a problem with her child's hearing or attention span. Instead of backing off, she redoubles her efforts with the best of intentions by talking to her child more loudly or moving into the girl's field of vision. This overwhelms the baby even more. She starts to cry, which makes the mother feel like a failure.

Once the parents understand that their child is showing them how much stimulation she can take at the moment, they begin to respond more appropriately. This breaks the cycle of frustration and allows the child to become more comfortable with her environment without feeling overwhelmed. It also helps the parents interpret their child's behavior as a reflection of her strengths instead of her weaknesses.

◆   ◆   ◆

HINTS FOR HANDLING A FRAGILE CHILD

If you have a premature baby or one who's fragile in some way, there are several things you can do to help channel your protective instincts most appropriately:

◆ Talk to your child's pediatrician about what your child can and cannot do. All too often, we pay much closer attention to the "cannots" than to the "cans." For example, many asthmatic children can participate fully in sports if the disease is being treated well. In fact, quite a few Olympic athletes over the past decade have had exercise-induced asthma. Some of the asthmatic children of a generation or two ago who were kept away from sports didn't have a chance to develop some of the social skills and self-confidence that their classmates learned.

Talk to your child's pediatrician not only about how her problem will affect her development, but also about how it won't. It's very reassuring to know that your newborn's colic, for example, has nothing to do with the relative weakness in her left arm. The colic will go away in a few months, just as it does with every other child who has it. (After all, how many teenagers do you know who still have colic?)

◆ Join a parents' support group. There are thousands of groups for parents of children who have physical problems. You can get information from your child's pediatrician or a local hospital.

Parents who enthusiastically seek help for their children often fail to seek help for themselves at the same time. By hearing how other parents tackle certain problems, and by sharing your own successes and failures, you can learn a lot. Listening to other parents in the same situation will often tell you if you're being overprotective. It may also tell you if you're so overwhelmed by what's going on that you're not being protective enough.

◆ Don't forget about the other children in your family. Sibling rivalry can be especially strong when the youngest child is ill. Preschoolers and young school-age children may worry that it's their fault that their younger sibling is sick.

Schedule time to spend alone with each of your other children. Let them know that those times are sacred— you won't allow anything to interrupt. Even a few minutes per week of your undivided attention will go a long way toward easing the rivalry.

◆   ◆   ◆

THE HIDDEN BENEFITS OF CUDDLING YOUR CHILD

Children respond very differently to being touched. As I mentioned earlier, some infants and toddlers are hypersensitive and easily overwhelmed by being stroked or cuddled. Others cling to their parents, showing an unquenchable thirst for affection and protection.

Recent studies have shown that touch can have a profound physiological effect on infants. We've known for years that baby laboratory rats who are kept away from their mothers have abnormally low levels of certain hormones. Those hormones return to near-normal levels, however, if the baby rats are stroked.

Those rat studies led Dr. Tiffany M. Field, a professor of psychology, psychiatry, and pediatrics at the University of Miami Medical School, to try some experiments with premature babies who were hospitalized in a neonatal intensive care unit. These are the high-risk babies whose care is very expensive and usually involves a lot of high-tech equipment. One measure of their overall health is the amount of weight they gain, both while they're in the hospital and when they're at home.

In addition to their normal treatment, Dr. Field had the nurses give some of the babies three fifteen-minute periods of gentle massage each day. What she found was extraordinary. The babies who received the massage grew 47 percent more while in the intensive care unit than those who did not. Their average hospital stay was shortened by six days, and their average hospital bill was three thousand dollars less than the other babies. One year later, their weights were still greater and they were better developed than the babies who weren't massaged.

So unless your baby becomes uncomfortable and tries to push away, don't worry that you're cuddling too much. That way, when she reaches adolescence and goes through a normal period of being terribly embarrassed even to be seen with you in public, you'll have some memories to tide you over until she comes around again.

INFANTS AND DISCIPLINE

When I speak to groups of parents, I sometimes get questions about the best way to discipline infants. I begin my answer by saying that discipline is teaching. (The words *discipline* and *disciple* have the same Latin root.) But to teach effectively, you have to understand how your child is thinking.

Although we now know infants can do much more than we had ever imagined, their thinking skills are extremely primitive, and will remain that way for several years. Even after they've started speaking, toddlers still can't understand abstract concepts like "danger"—so verbal warnings are useless. Parents of precocious children sometimes forget this. They'll tell their child, who's lunging at their household pet with outstretched hands, "Now, don't poke the cat in the eye. Remember, Bobby, don't poke!" Bobby hears the words and replies, "Don't poke!"

His parents think this means their young son understands their warning. In fact, he's only mimicking the last part of what he heard. They soon discover this when they hear first the cat and then Bobby scream. Sure enough, he tried to poke the cat in the eye, and was quickly scratched for his efforts.

Warning, spanking, and threatening infants are not only completely ineffective as ways to discipline them, they're counterproductive. *The only way to discipline a baby is to protect him from his natural curiosity and lack of judgment.*

This is known as environmental control. If you don't want your baby to stick his fingers in the electrical outlets, you'll have to put safety caps on those outlets. If you don't want him to drink poisonous cleaning fluids, you'll have to keep all cleaning supplies in a locked cabinet. Your baby has absolutely no way of knowing how dangerous something might be. In fact, the very concept of danger is too abstract for him to understand. All he knows is that these, like so many other things, look attractive and he wants to explore them.

That also means that your baby never does things because he's out to get you—even though it may feel that way at times. Willful disobedience is also too abstract and complex for him to understand. Whenever you think your baby is being spiteful, look for another reason to explain his behavior, such as hunger or too much stimulation.

Once you understand what's going on, you can use your child's natural desire to explore new things to your advantage. Many parents of older babies dislike going to the grocery store or supermarket with them because their babies fuss and cry. One common reason for that fussiness is that they're frustrated as they sit in the back of the shopping cart. They see all these brightly colored boxes, cans, and fruit, but can't touch them.

What my wife and I did with our son, which worked very well, was to begin each shopping trip by giving him something we were going to buy that he could hold and explore. We chose things that were brightly colored (an orange) or that made noise (a box of cereal), but that he couldn't destroy and that weren't dangerous if he accidentally opened them. Each of these items kept him amused for a minute or two as we cruised through the store and finished our shopping.

As soon as he became bored and started reaching for something on a shelf, we'd give him a new item to hold and put the old one back in the cart. The only other thing we had to do was keep the cart in the center of the aisle so that he couldn't actually reach any of the shelves if we didn't spot his boredom in time. By using environmental control, we turned a potentially aggravating experience into an outing that was occasionally even fun.

◆   ◆   ◆

WHY HITTING A CHILD ISN'T EFFECTIVE DISCIPLINE

While no rational person believes in beating children to control them, I've spoken with some very intelligent parents and child-care providers who felt it was appropriate to slap or otherwise hit young children—including infants—to discipline them.

Every parent occasionally gets furious at his or her children. There were times—mostly when I was sleep-deprived and trying to meet a deadline for my work—when I had brief thoughts of hitting my infant son if he didn't stop crying or wouldn't go to sleep. An acquaintance of mine, who's a child psychoanalyst and used to be the director of psychiatry training at a major medical center on the east coast, told me during a moment of particular candor how he used to picture himself strangling his colicky newborn son when the child's screaming and crying went on for hours.

There's nothing unusual or wrong about those fantasies—although parents seldom discuss them in public.

What's important is that we never act on them. You shouldn't be surprised if you find yourself having similar thoughts. If you feel you may lose control, and there's someone else to care for your baby for a while, take a break. You can also call a local or national crisis phone line (there's usually at least one such number listed on the inside front cover of your local white pages telephone book) so that you can get some help ventilating your feelings without endangering your child or yourself.

Sometimes, however, adults hit children out of ignorance. I once was talking with a college student I knew who did a lot of baby-sitting for several families, including mine. She told me that whenever a baby or toddler she was caring for did something bad, she would slap his hand hard and then tell him what he was doing wrong. She saw this as an effective, educational approach. I asked her to extend her right hand and, when she did, I slapped it hard enough that it stung for a second. She was taken aback.

"That hurts, and it makes you angry, doesn't it?" I asked.

"Why, yes," she replied.

"Right now, you're concentrating on how angry you are at me for doing such a thing. That anger makes you less receptive to what I'm saying, since you're primed for an argument. You want to get even with me, maybe even destroy me."

She thought about that for a second, and realized how angry she really was.

"That's how a child feels when you slap him. He's concentrating on his anger so much that he's not ready to learn anything else for a while. By hitting the child, you're making things worse, not better. The next time you feel the urge to hit, just slap your own hand instead," I said. I also gave her some books to read on discipline, and showed her some techniques that work a lot better with young children.

◆   ◆   ◆

A FEW WORDS ABOUT TWINS, TRIPLETS, AND . . .

Several months ago, after I gave a speech in Baltimore, two women approached me with a question. They were obviously uncomfortable as they glanced at each other, each encouraging the other to be brave and speak first.

Finally, one of them cleared her throat and said, "Uh, Dr. Kutner, I have quadruplets and my friend over there has triplets, and we'd like to talk to you about sibling rivalry!"

Parents of what are known as "multiples" face special challenges. Multiple births have long been associated with myths and superstitions. They have been used as symbols for good and evil. The director of a social service agency for families with multiple births told me that she gets calls from some parents when their children are a few days old, saying that they already know which is the "bad" twin. The idea that one twin will be evil is total nonsense, of course. But it shows how powerful and ingrained these myths are.

About one of every eighty births results in twins. About one of every three sets of twins is identical—they have the same genetic makeup. The remainder are fraternal, and are no more alike genetically than other brothers and sisters.

To the parents who raise them, twins bring a special set of frustrations, challenges, and rewards. The relationship between twins is both a bond and a rivalry that begins in the womb and lasts until they die.

Identical twins can have uncanny skills at communicating with each other. During infancy and toddlerhood, they may even develop their own primitive language.

Studies of twins have shown that some of the things our own parents tended to do with twins and triplets put them at risk for later problems. Until the 1970s, parents and professionals tended to treat twins as a single unit instead of as individuals. Twins were often dressed alike and given similar names that emphasized their special relationship. But there's evidence that paying little attention to twins' differences can delay their physical and emotional development, and possibly lead to a lower IQ score.

Other studies have found that the older siblings of twins can feel a great deal of stress following their birth. Not only are the other children facing the normal rivalries they'd feel with the birth of any child, they're angry at the extra attention twins receive. Older single children quickly realize that twinship is one area in which they can never compete, which makes them even more jealous of the new arrivals.

◆   ◆   ◆

HINTS FOR PARENTS
OF MULTIPLES

Researchers who study families with twins and triplets have found several things that parents can do from the beginning that will help their children develop fully. Remember that twins will naturally feel a special closeness. Some of the things parents used to do to emphasize the relationship wound up causing problems later on.

◆ Pay extra attention to the names you give your children. It used to be the fashion to give twins related names like Mary Sue and Mary Jo. Keep in mind that names have a strong influence on how others respond to children as individuals. By giving them similar names, you'll be encouraging family members and, later on, teachers to ignore your children's individual personalities and strengths. Similar names may also make it more difficult for the children themselves to develop individual identities.

◆ Encourage family members and other adults not to refer to them as "the twins." Calling them by one name belittles their distinctiveness and, when they get older, may make them feel they're not being accorded the same respect as the other children in their family or classroom.

When they enter toddlerhood, be sure to give them social experiences both together and apart. That will help their friends and teachers see them more easily as individuals. It will also allow them to take advantage of their special relationship without becoming inappropriately dependent on each other.

♦ From the beginning, give friends and family members ways of telling them apart if they're identical twins. That can be as simple as parting their hair on opposite sides (assuming they have hair when they're born!). Dressing them in different wardrobes can make a big difference in the way identical twins are treated by outsiders.

♦ Allow each of the twins to have his or her own special possessions. Don't force them to share everything. This doesn't mean that you have to buy two of every stuffed animal. After all, they'll end up trading every toy and piece of clothing they own by the time they're a few years old. But it's important as they enter toddlerhood that they each know certain objects are theirs and not their twin's. They need to feel that they can really possess something before they can be comfortable sharing anything. Forcing them to share everything will bring out their innate competitiveness.

♦   ♦   ♦

CHAPTER 8

The Importance of
Temperament

During the first month of life, his temperament is embodied in
his reflexes—in how often he cries, how quickly he stops crying, whether he flails or cuddles while he is being held.
—DAPHNE MAURER, PH.D., AND CHARLES MAURER[1]

Days or even hours after their children are born, parents
reach conclusions about their temperaments. They may describe their babies as fussy or easygoing, sensitive or curious.

For years, pediatricians and psychologists paid little attention to parents' very early descriptions of their babies, chalk-
ing them up to wishful thinking or naïveté. Newborn infants
were regarded as little more than a collection of reflexes. They
were blank slates, primitive organisms that required time for
their personalities to develop in response to their environments.

But in recent years, researchers have discovered that the
parents were right all along! The early patterns of crying,
cooing, shyness, response to stimulation, and perhaps even
the frequency of the kicks before a baby is born appear to

---

[1]D. Maurer and C. Maurer, *The World of the Newborn* (New York: Basic
Books, 1988), p. 225.

offer parents valuable information about the ways children will approach life as they grow older.

Temperament is a deceptively difficult concept. Think of it as a description of *how* a child reacts to the world around him—the child's personal style and sensitivities—as opposed to why he reacts that way or what specific behaviors parents see. For example, all babies become startled and cry at times, but some do it in many situations and others in only a few.

There's a wide variation in how much stimulation it takes to trigger such crying. Some babies seem to be especially sensitive to changes in temperature. They become very upset if they wear certain pieces of clothing. They have unpredictable eating and sleeping patterns, and seem to be generally disgruntled and mad at the world.

Other babies seem to take all these changes in stride. You know exactly when they'll eat, sleep, and need their diapers changed. Most of the time they're in a pretty good mood.

These patterns in the differences in children's behavior are reflections of their temperaments. Researchers have found that temperaments are fairly consistent over time. A calm baby is likely to turn into a relatively calm toddler, adolescent, and adult. A baby who has difficulty with transitions will probably have similar difficulties, though not necessarily as dramatic, throughout her life. They've also found that the temperaments of identical twins are more similar, on average, than the temperaments of fraternal twins, indicating that at least part of what's going on is genetic.

Even though these temperaments are pretty stable, they are not immutable. In fact, parents and children tend to become more like each other in temperament over time, but the changes are so small that parents may not notice them from year to year.

The other critically important aspect of temperament is goodness of fit. Some children fit into certain families or environments much better than others. This isn't just a matter of everyone having the same temperament. In fact, parents who were shy as children and have overcome that problem may have a lot of difficulty with a child who is shy. They feel her pain too greatly.

Dr. Stanley Turecki,[2] a child psychiatrist in New York who specializes in helping the families of children who have "difficult" temperaments, loves to give the example of a five-year-old girl who's a very active tomboy and lives with three older brothers on a farm in the midwestern United States. That child is likely to be considered normal and not much of a problem. She can fit her temperament to her environment.

But if you take that same girl and make her the daughter of two older, fussy parents who live in a cramped city apartment and send her to a highly structured private school, she'll probably be labeled "hyperactive" and a troublemaker within a week.

Always remember that a child doesn't have to be average to be normal. Children with very different temperaments can be equally successful.

◆   ◆   ◆

WHAT'S YOUR BABY'S TEMPERAMENT?

It's often interesting to figure out how professionals would characterize your baby's temperament. If you feel that you're having a lot of difficulty coping with your new baby, answering these questions can often help you get a handle on where the stress points might be.

But first, some background. Perhaps the most famous research on temperament is the New York Longitudinal Study, which was begun in 1956 and has followed 133 people from infancy to adulthood. It's still going on.

This study defined nine temperamental traits, all of which can be spotted during infancy—although not necessarily within the first few months after birth:

◆ **Activity level.** Is your baby generally squirmy and

2Dr. Turecki is the author of a very useful book about temperaments called *The Difficult Child* (New York: Bantam, 1989).

active, or relaxed and laid back? (There's some evidence that very active newborns are the ones that mothers complained about as kicking a lot before they were born.)

♦ **Regularity.** How predictable are your baby's eating and sleeping cycles?

♦ **Approach/withdrawal.** How does your baby respond to new situations and people? Does she brighten when she sees something new, or does she recoil?

♦ **Adaptability.** How well does your baby handle changes in her schedule or minor disruptions of her activities? If she becomes upset, does she recover quickly?

♦ **Sensory threshold.** How sensitive is your baby to bright lights, loud noises or scratchy clothes?

♦ **Mood.** Does your baby appear to be basically happy or generally upset and angry?

♦ **Intensity.** How loud is your baby when she's either excited or unhappy? Does she seem extroverted or subdued?

♦ **Distractibility.** If your baby is hungry, for example, can you stop her crying temporarily by talking to her quietly or giving her a pacifier?

♦ **Persistence.** Does your baby play with a simple toy for a long time, or does she prefer to go quickly from toy to toy?

Thinking about your baby's temperament in these terms may give you clues to solving some of the behavior problems that you find especially frustrating. Remember, you're simply looking at your child's behaviors. You're not trying to ascribe motives to those behaviors. ("She's doing this to get my goat!")

If, for example, your baby has a low sensory threshold, you may notice that she startles and cries when a radio or a light in her room is turned on. But the signs may be more subtle than that. She might reject a bottle because it's too warm or too cold. She might push away from you or scream when you pick her up because she's so sensitive to touch.

Sometimes babies like this can make parents do what would be right for other children, but is exactly the wrong thing to do for them. For example, if you're trying to rock

118 LAWRENCE KUTNER, PH.D.

a baby who has a very low sensory threshold to sleep, you may actually be making matters worse as you try to make them better, since the rocking may stimulate instead of soothe her. In extreme cases, even singing your baby a lullaby may get her too excited to sleep. The problem gets worse, of course, when your baby cries because she's overstimulated, and you try to calm her by singing yet another lullaby.

It's easy to misinterpret these children's behaviors, or not to see them as linked by temperament. But once you recognize the pattern, you can begin to help her out. If she's easily overwhelmed, begin by decreasing the visual, auditory, and tactile stimulation in her room. See if any of the toys in her crib are so exciting that they get her "wound up."

Try to find out which textures or materials in her clothes or diapers might be irritating her. (You might try changing laundry detergents or eliminating the fabric softener you're using.) Think about purchasing window blinds that are more lightproof if that's what's bothering her. You might even try a "white noise" generator like an electric fan. Keep experimenting to see what works.

◆　　◆　　◆

COPING WITH A DIFFICULT TEMPERAMENT

There can be striking differences between the temperaments of siblings. One mother I interviewed was totally distraught over her newborn son's behavior. From the day he was born, her older son had behaved as if he had been studying Dr. Spock in the womb. She felt as if she knew exactly when he would want to eat and nap and need his diaper changed. Within a week or two he was sleeping through the night. He seemed calm and happy most of the time.

When her second son was born three and a half years later, she expected the same things. Instead, her younger son spent much of the day fussing and crying inconsolably. He never slept for more than two hours at a time. He rejected breast-feeding in favor of formula from a bottle—an act that his mother interpreted as a personal rejection as well. (She described his eating during those first few weeks as so voracious that "he would work up a sweat" before gulping down the last ounce of the bottle.)

"I thought I would go nuts," she said. "Once, at three A.M., after a night of his constantly wanting to be fed and held, I completely broke down and cried, 'Please let me sleep!' "

This mother's reaction to the stresses of caring for a newborn—especially a very demanding newborn—were perfectly normal. Yet like her, many parents are shocked and dismayed by the intensity of their anger and frustration. New parents seldom talk about these emotions, which tend to be glossed over even when more experienced parents warn new ones about how little sleep they will get.

As I mentioned in Chapter 7, parents' feelings of anger and frustration during the first two months are both normal and predictable. The child is demanding a great deal and giving very little back in terms of social interaction like giggling and cooing. The parents are usually exhausted and not in the best physical or emotional shape to deal with the extra stress.

All of these problems are compounded when the child's temperament makes him more difficult. Most newborns don't develop predictable patterns in their eating or sleeping for at least a couple of weeks. Temperamentally difficult children may have even more erratic schedules that take longer to fall into a pattern that allows other family members to get on with their own lives.

These infants may cry more often or seem to cry more intensely than other babies. Nothing seems to calm them down. Sometimes this is because the parents are paying attention to the wrong things. If their baby is sensitive to certain types of clothing that he's wearing or is very sensitive to being touched at all, trying to comfort him by stroking his back will only make things worse. That's why parents of these babies can help themselves by doing some of the detective work I described in the last box.

It's a good idea to check with books and with other parents about how reasonable your expectations are for your baby's behavior. For example, remember that the amount of daily crying a baby does almost always increases during the first six weeks. Parents who don't understand this are likely to interpret the growing amount of crying as a sign that something is wrong—either with their baby or with them.

Dr. Edward Christophersen, the chief of behavioral pediatrics at Children's Mercy Hospital in Kansas City, Missouri, studied the babies who had been diagnosed by their parents as having colic, and brought to the hospital's clinic for treatment.

Most parents have heard of colic, and know that the babies who have it cry a lot. Colic is a problem that appears to be related to the baby's immature digestive system. A colicky baby will show very specific symptoms aside from crying. Soon after a meal he'll suddenly clench his fists, draw his legs up to his abdomen, and start crying in pain. The crying can last for hours. Although it can be dramatic, colic isn't dangerous. It almost always clears up by the time babies are three months old.

But when Dr. Christophersen and the clinic pediatricians examined the babies whose parents thought they had colic, they found that 35 percent of those babies had absolutely nothing wrong with them. Their patterns of crying were perfectly normal—but they were different from what the parents had expected. Since those parents didn't know how much crying was normal, they assumed their child was sick.

♦   ♦   ♦

LOOKING AT LIFE FROM THE BABY'S POINT OF VIEW

One way to cut down on the problems you'll have with your newborn over the first few months is to look at things from your baby's point of view. Parents who are very frustrated often find themselves attributing adult motives to their baby's behaviors. ("He's disappointed in me!" "She's out to get me!")

Here are some tips to help you realign your perspective on life as a new parent:

♦ Try not to "awfulize." That's a made-up word a colleague of mine uses to describe the pattern many new parents fall into when they're sleep-deprived, frustrated, and depressed—the normal state of affairs. It's so easy during those first few months to think that the problems will never end. You feel as if your son will never sleep through the night, will always spit up food after eating, and will never learn to smile—even though you don't know any adults or even older children who still act this way.

Instead, try to remember what you do when you're driving a car. You don't look at the road that's only a few feet ahead of you. If you did that, you wouldn't have time to react to problems and you'd never know where you were. Instead, you look farther down the road so that you can anticipate the changes ahead. You can do the same thing to gain a sense of perspective with your children.

♦ Don't take your baby's behavior personally. Remember that having a healthy baby who cries a lot or doesn't sleep or eat well for the first few months is seldom a sign that you're doing something wrong. It's largely the luck of the draw as to what type of temperament your child has.

Because few parents—and grandparents—understand the subtleties of temperament, you may have to be prepared to shrug off occasionally accusatory comments and help them learn what's really going on.

♦ Look for subtle changes in your child's behavior. This is related to changing your sense of perspective. For example, although your baby is probably crying more at six weeks of age than at two weeks, the time of the crying is probably more predictable. (Most babies cry more in the evening than during the day.)

This means that even though your baby is crying more, her schedule is showing how her nervous system is developing. By being sensitive to this changing pattern, you will be more prepared and less frustrated by your child's fussing.

♦ Try to work with your child's temperament. Remember the detective work you need to do to figure out what's getting your baby so upset. If you have a sensitive, jumpy baby, you may need to curb your natural enthusiasm and approach your child in a slower, softer, gentler way.

♦   ♦   ♦

FOCUSING ON THE
OTHER RELATIONSHIP

No matter how sweet and easygoing your baby's temperament is, she'll put a tremendous strain on your relationship with your spouse. For the first few months, you may be more exhausted than you've ever been in your lives. Tempers flare. Depression sets in. You feel overwhelmed. Knowing that these dramatic feelings are normal helps somewhat. But it's also important to anticipate some of the stresses you'll face. That's why I included that questionnaire in Chapter 1.

With all the attention paid to your new baby, it's easy for your own feelings and needs to get lost in the shuffle. Although all parents engage in some self-sacrifice for their children, keep in mind that your goal isn't just to raise a happy, healthy child. You want that child to be part of a happy, healthy family as well.

For that to happen, you'll have to focus some of your energy on your spouse and yourself. The strains of parenthood are more easily borne when you feel that you're supported in your relationship with your husband or wife.

If you step back and think about all the changes you've undergone over the past year, you may discover that you've let some of the important patterns in your life disappear. How often do you talk about things *besides* the baby? When was the last time you went to a movie or to a restaurant that didn't serve fast food? How recently have you traded back rubs with each other? What other little rituals have you lost?

◆   ◆   ◆

TIPS FOR REBUILDING YOUR RELATIONSHIP

Taking some time for yourselves as a couple—away from your baby—can help make you better and more patient parents. The same holds for taking some time to be alone. As a new parent, it sometimes feels as if the only time you may have alone is when your baby's asleep and you're trying to do exactly the same.

Often, you don't need more than a few minutes at a time to recharge your emotional batteries. Here are some ideas:

◆ See if a neighbor or family member will baby-sit, even if only for fifteen minutes so that you can take a walk around the block either alone or with your spouse. It's easy to get "cabin fever" if you're cooped up all day at home. Just breathing some fresh air can help you feel revitalized.

◆ If you can get away for an hour or more with your spouse, go somewhere quiet where you can talk and eat a snack. But don't go to the movies—it's hard to reestablish communication if you're both sitting quietly and looking at someone else.

◆ Plan a schedule of "relief hours" with one or two other new parents from your neighborhood. For example, you might arrange with two other couples for one set of you to watch all three babies for an hour or so every Thursday evening, so that the others can get some time together. The responsibility for baby-sitting would rotate from week to week.

◆   ◆   ◆

C H A P T E R 9

Growth and Coordination

Toward the end of the first year of life, when they learn to clamber to their feet, they're celebrating that period millions of years ago when our ancestors got up off all fours. . , , Our ancestors stood up because they had found more useful things to do with their hands than walking on them.
—BENJAMIN SPOCK, M.D., AND
MICHAEL B. ROTHENBERG, M.D.[1]

THE DANCE OF DEVELOPMENT

It's a shame we can't directly watch our babies' brains and nervous systems grow, seeing the pathways develop and the connections made. We can, however, get indirect glimpses at what's going on by paying attention to our children's development—especially their physical development. The patterns and increasing complexity of their coordination show us how they are wiring their own brains for later life as they master control of their bodies and their environment. With only a little imagination, you can see in your child a com-

[1]B. Spock and M. B. Rothenberg, Dr. Spock's Baby and Child Care (New York: Pocket Books, 1992), p. 301.

125

pressed history of the evolution of human beings as a species.[2]

The first steps in this dance of physical development are the reflexes, which I described earlier. Many of these, such as the walking and tonic neck reflexes, will disappear within the first few months, just as other physical skills begin to develop. While most books on child development describe each aspect of a child's coordination separately, I find it more useful to see how they interact, and how a child uses diverse skills to his advantage. Keep in mind that the ages I use in these descriptions are approximations. Don't worry if your baby takes a little longer.

When you look at your newborn baby, one of the first things you'll probably notice is that, compared to an adult or even a toddler, his head is disproportionately large. Also, your baby's neck is still quite weak. (That's why it's so important always to support a newborn's head and *never* to shake a baby.) If you watch carefully, you'll find that during the first month he'll only be able to raise his head briefly while he's lying down. At two months, his neck muscles have strengthened enough to hold his head up longer while he's lying on his belly, and also to hold it up while he's sitting. (Of course, he'll need your help with the sitting part.) A few weeks later he'll probably not only hold his head up while he's lying down, but he'll look around a little bit.

All of this is coordinated with how well he uses his hands. We've seen ultrasound images of fetuses sucking their thumbs or their fists, apparently for comfort, so it's not surprising that many newborns can do that right away—although some may need your help finding their mouths with their thumbs the first few times. But controlled use of their

[2]Much has been written about this, often invoking the phrase "ontogeny recapitulates phylogeny." In other words, the development of a baby starting with the fertilized egg appears to act out, in a highly compressed form, certain aspects of the evolutionary history of human beings as a species. That means that some of the apparently very small and subtle skills your baby is learning over the course of a week or a month may have taken tens of thousands of years of our evolution to develop.

hands to grab and release something (as opposed to the un-controlled grasp of the palmar reflex) doesn't come for a few months. By the time they're three months old, most children will coordinate their new head control and hand control skills so that they can grab or playfully swipe at rattles and other objects that interest them.

All of this exercise strengthens your baby's arms enough that, by the fourth or fifth month, he can probably lift both his head and his chest off the surface he's lying on. This is great fun for your baby, and quite an accomplishment. He also is kicking with his legs more. By combining the two at random, one day at this age he'll suddenly find himself rolling over onto his side or back.

Once he's tasted success at rolling over, he appears driven to repeat his accomplishment. The problem is, he may not remember exactly what he did. So he tries more movements, looking for the ones that will flip him over.

This period of physical coordination marks a new stage in the relationship between you and your child. Until now, he has been active but immobile. If you put him in one position on his crib or on the floor, and came back a minute later, you could be sure he'd still be exactly where and how you'd left him. But now he not only has a will of his own, but the coordination to express at least some of that will through movement.

In other words, he can now get himself into trouble. It's at this age that you have to be particularly careful about leaving your baby alone on the changing table or on a bed. He now has the strength and coordination to roll off, but not the foresight to prevent it.

He's also working on his balance. By about six months, your baby will probably be able to sit up—that is to say, he can stay in a seated position by himself, using his arms for support. Soon he can balance for a short while without using his arms.

This is a good thing since, while all this is going on with his head and neck, your baby is also getting more sophisticated in how he grasps small objects. He'll begin to use his thumb to grasp something by pressing it against his palm. It will be a few more months before he shifts to using it in coordination with his fingers. This change of less than an inch is what allows him to pick up and manipulate small toys and pieces of solid food with a great deal of control. It is the first step toward feeding himself. It also allows him to play with things in more interesting ways while he's sitting.

About this time, he'll begin working on improving his mobility, probably through creeping and crawling. (The difference between the two is that your baby's belly stays on the ground during creeping, but comes off the ground while crawling.) This, too, comes about in stages. If you watch closely, you'll probably see your baby lift himself off the floor on his hands and knees, and rock back and forth. He's probably still too weak at first to lift one of his limbs in this position, so the rocking serves as a muscle-strengthening exercise.

After enough practice rocking, one day he'll lift up one of his arms or legs and put it in a new position. He's moved! It's an incredible experience. But like most quantum leaps in his coordination and physical development, he may not remember exactly what he did to accomplish it. You may find him repeatedly lifting a hand or knee, and then putting it back in the same place instead of moving forward. After a few practice sessions, he'll get the hang of it.

I've always been impressed by the different paths babies take in their physical development on the way to walking. It's rare to see a behavior that starts out with such wide natural variation, yet becomes so uniform after only a few months. In other words, any given toddler's style of walking is very close to any other's. But when they were babies, one may have crawled mostly backward while the other went forward or scooted about in his own idiosyncratic way. No one approach appears to be that much better than any other. (It's a wonderful image, though, if you picture this diversity continuing through adulthood. Some people would walk forward, some backward, and still others might hop or skip to get to their destinations.)

Another way your baby is strengthening his muscles is by pulling himself up to a standing position in his crib or by holding on to a piece of furniture. This usually happens at about nine months, and reflects your child's improved grasp, better balance, and greater leg and arm strength. Don't be surprised if, during this initial learning period, you find your baby standing, but obviously very upset or even crying. Usually, that's because he's mastered the act of standing up, but hasn't figured out how to get back down again. He doesn't yet realize that he has to bend his knees. Give him some help by bending them for him. He may plop down on his backside, but he'll be delighted. In fact, he may amuse himself by bobbing up and down for a half hour or longer at a time.

Once he's figured out how to stand up while holding on to something, he'll probably begin what's known as cruising— walking unsteadily from one piece of furniture to another while holding on to them for balance.

The next step (quite literally) is walking. Those first steps are unsteady, with the feet forming a wide base for stability and his arms outstretched for balance. Despite their awkwardness, they are a thing of beauty to any parent who sees them, for they are the culmination of a year of intense athletic training and determination. By the time your baby is roughly a year old, he has mastered the physical coordination he will use throughout his life. From now on, it's all a matter of refining those skills.

◆   ◆   ◆

A FEW NOTES ON SAFETY

You won't have to worry about your baby's safety very much until he can crawl. Still, some of the things you buy and do even before he's born can help make your home much safer for him. While a great deal of safety information is common sense (e.g., don't feed him something he might choke on, don't leave electrical outlets uncapped, etc.), some of the most important steps you can take toward safety are much more subtle. While the topic is worthy of an entire book—and there are, in fact, several excellent books on child safety on the market—here's a quick rundown of some of the things you might forget.

♦ Buy an infant car seat. As I mentioned earlier I can't stress this enough. Regular seat belts don't work well for infants and toddlers, and in fact can be dangerous to them.

♦ Check which plants you have at home. Unfortunately, many decorative household plants are poisonous. And while you know not to nibble on them, an inquisitive baby won't. The two most likely offenders are philodendron and dieffenbachia, but there are others, especially those associated with Christmas such as holly berries, mistletoe, and poinsettia, that few parents give second thoughts to.

♦ Turn down your water heater if you can. This will decrease the likelihood of your accidentally scalding your baby when you draw the water for his bath.

♦ If you're buying or being given used baby furniture, find out the latest safety specifications from the local office of the U.S. Consumer Products Safety Commission (a federal agency with offices in most major cities) to see if the old furniture measures up.

For example, the current standard for the space between the vertical slats on a crib is that they be no more than 2⅜ inches apart—smaller than any baby's head. Some older cribs have slats set wider apart, which can lead to a baby getting his head caught. Also, make sure that your crib doesn't have any decorative posts sticking up at the headboard or footboard. Some older infants have accidentally strangled when part of their clothing became caught on such posts.

♦ Use safety devices, but don't rely on them. I know that sounds like a strange statement, but you shouldn't become complacent about your baby's safety just because he's in a high chair or you're using a safety belt on a changing table. You can't leave your child alone and assume he'll stay put.

Each year, about fourteen hundred babies in the United States are taken to hospital emergency rooms because of falls from changing tables. In 1989, more than seventy-five hundred children were taken to hospitals because of injuries related to high chairs. In both cases, some of the children had managed to squirm out of their safety straps while their parents weren't looking.

◆ Be careful with certain solid foods. Never feed honey to an infant who's under a year old, since he runs the risk of getting infant botulism, a type of food poisoning. That risk disappears around the child's first birthday.

Other foods present choking hazards. Never feed a baby nuts (including peanuts), hard candies, whole grapes, raw carrots, or hot dogs, all of which are routinely associated with choking. You can decrease the risk of the grapes and hot dogs by slicing them in quarters lengthwise before cutting them into bite-size bits.

◆   ◆   ◆

THE EMOTIONS OF TOYS

Toys play an integral part in babies' developing physical coordination. These days, parents hear a tremendous amount about how specific toys can help children master specific tasks. Unfortunately, much of this is overblown, with more of an eye toward marketing than child development. I'll talk more about this in Chapter 12. But for now, let's look at some of the real connections between toys and your child's physical coordination.

A friend of mine, who's an avid sailboat racer, once told me that if I wanted to see what that sport was really like, all I had to do was stand under a cold shower for an hour and tear up hundred-dollar bills. Needless to say, he wasn't a parent, or he would have known that the site of the true bottomless financial pit is the toy store. It's amazing how much a few pieces of plastic and paper will sell for if the purchasers are parents or grandparents, especially when the manufacturers claim their product improves a child's intellectual or physical development.[3]

It's easy to be manipulated into buying expensive and worthless toys for our own children. After all, it's seldom a rational decision. On one side is the pressure from the toy companies. "Buy this mobile and your baby's intellect will soar," they imply in their ads. "Buy this rattle and improve your child's physical coordination." Now, what kind of parent would you be if you didn't care about your child's cognitive and physical development?—even if the link between a particular toy and brain growth is tenuous, to say the least.

On the other side are our own memories and unfulfilled wishes. Will we give our children, even at this young an age, those things we wished we'd had as children? Toys sometimes become a symbolic way of filling the emotional holes from our own past. From your child's perspective, the twenty-dollar version of a toy may not be any better than the five-dollar one, but as parents, we may wish to give our children only "the best." The problem is, when it comes to a child's development, the most expensive isn't always the best.

A few weeks ago I was in a fancy toy store, looking at what was available and trying out a few of them myself. A lot of parents in the store were doing the same thing, including one couple who wouldn't let their five-year-old son play with the remote-controlled fire truck because they were having so much fun with it themselves!

I told the clerk that I was looking for a set of large corrugated cardboard blocks for a toddler. Nothing could be simpler, I thought, as he disappeared into a back room. Moments later he came out with a box that was half as tall as he was

---

[3] Bear in mind that with a healthy young baby, it's seldom useful to differentiate between physical and intellectual development since the two go hand in hand. Toys that help a baby practice a physical skill will usually help with a cognitive one as well.

(and he was a very big guy), and just as wide and deep. It was filled with color-coded plastic blocks about the size of bricks, as well as what he called "interlocking stabilization attachments," otherwise known as plastic bolts and nuts.

I told him that the set was much more extensive than I'd envisioned and, in any event, it was too complicated for a young toddler. "Oh no," he said. "This is perfect, even for children less than a year old. It will help develop their coordination."

He told me that this was the best block set available, that it was his store's exclusively, and that my child (for whom he assumed I was buying the blocks) would thank me for getting it. He then started to describe how much fun we'd have building large forts together and playing in them.

I was having trouble restraining myself from laughing. He obviously had no idea what an infant could do, and he sounded like a stereotype used-car salesman trying to sell me an Edsel. I asked him how much the block set cost. "Only three hundred dollars!" he said. "And it's our last one."

What blatant manipulation! The blocks were so complicated that a preschooler might have difficulty with them, never mind a baby who's barely past learning how to stack one thing on top of another. In fact, a set of blocks this complex would probably be counterproductive to a child's developing physical coordination and self-confidence, since it would lead to frustration in both the parent and the child—especially since the parent had been told by an "expert" that the child was the right age for the toy.

But what really impressed me was that the salesman had managed to interweave guilt, fantasy, love, and gratitude into the purchase of a simple set of blocks. It was no longer a toy, but a measure of how much I valued the child. Needless to say, I declined to buy it.

◆   ◆   ◆

TOYS TO GROW ON

I don't want to imply that I'm against toys. Quite the contrary. Toys are the equipment in your baby's laboratory, the tools through which she discovers how the world works, and practices her developing physical and intellectual skills. It's very important that your baby have adequate tools for that exploration.

What I am against, however, are overpriced toys that bear false promises about what they'll do for your child. And I'm concerned about cheap but dangerous toys that could harm your baby.

Luckily, there are many toys that you can either make at home or that are made for other purposes, which are very inexpensive and will thrill your baby. If you try some of these toys instead of buying their overpriced, prepackaged equivalents, you'll save up to several hundred dollars. I'll give you some ideas, but the most fun comes from developing them yourself.

Keep a few rules in mind when you do this. Obviously, any toy for a baby should have no sharp edges and shouldn't have any pieces that could break off. Also, remember that babies put everything in their mouths. Nothing should be so small that a child could accidentally swallow or choke on it. Although the federal government has specifications for toy sizes based on the diameter of young children's windpipes, I use a simpler and more conservative rule: nothing smaller than a golf ball for the first year.

Kitchen equipment is endlessly fascinating to children. It's one of the most popular categories of toys for toddlers and preschoolers, probably because the kitchen is the center of family life in many homes, and cooking is one of the activities a young child sees her parents doing. But for babies, the fact that the implements are used in preparing food is irrelevant. The shapes and actions are inherently intriguing. They also allow your child to practice eye-hand coordination and to explore concepts like "smaller" and "larger."

Once you see your baby is learning to pick things up with her fingers, buy her an inexpensive set of plastic dry measuring cups. They're rugged; she can chew on them; and they both nest and stack—two activities she'll love to try.

Unopened cans of cat food are also great for stacking (especially if you also have a cat). So are some cans of tuna. The lip on the top helps them interlock and makes them more stable than other types of cans when your child puts one on top of another.

Plastic measuring spoons are also a wonderful and inexpensive toy. If they're connected at one end, make sure the connection is secure and is too big to be swallowed.

A plastic bulb baster, such as a turkey baster, is a lot of fun since it's easy for a baby to squeeze. You may want to remove the cylinder, however.

Empty plastic soft-drink bottles are also great toys for helping your baby practice her coordination at picking things up. (They also make great noises when they're dropped, she'll soon discover.)

Brightly colored squares of cloth one- to three-feet on edge make wonderful toys. You can also use one of your old T-shirts or a receiving blanket. After your baby's about six months old, you can try hiding things underneath the cloth, such as a large ball or an old-fashioned windup clock that ticks. She'll delight in "discovering" the hidden treasures.

You're actually doing two things here: Covering and uncovering the object with the cloth takes physical coordination; knowing to look for the object under the cloth requires a recognition that objects still exist, even when they're out of sight (object permanence).

Cardboard mailing tubes and the cores from rolls of paper towels or toilet paper make fabulous toys for babies. Be sure to throw them out, however, before they're chewed through. Show your baby how a Ping-Pong ball or cloth napkin can go in one end of the tube and come

out the other—another way of playing with the concept
of object permanence. (Be careful that your baby doesn't
try to swallow the ball.)

There are many other inexpensive or even free toys
that your baby can use in her "laboratory," including:

♦ Empty boxes (small ones for stacking and large ones
for tunnels to crawl through).

♦ A piece of felt with circles, triangles, and rectangles
of contrasting colors sewn to it, or with bells (make sure
they're too large to swallow) sewn to it.

♦ Wooden kitchen spoons and empty coffee cans.

The best part about coming up with your own im-
promptu toys for your baby is that it encourages you to
watch her development more closely. You'll pay more
attention to when she learns to control the items she
grasps in her fingers, and when she begins looking for
objects that are out of her sight. That, in turn, will better
allow you to share in her sense of joy as she learns how
the world works.

♦   ♦   ♦

CHAPTER 10

To Sleep Like
a Baby

In many homes bedtime is bedlam time, with the children and
mother forming a mutual frustration society.
                                    —HAIM GINOTT, PH.D.[1]

If I had to bet on what type of problem you were to complain
about as you and your child got to know each other over the
first few weeks, I'd guess that it would have something to do
with sleep. Dr. Richard Ferber, the director of the center for
pediatric sleep disorders at Children's Hospital in Boston,
estimates that one of every four children will have significant
difficulty sleeping at some point. Hundreds of times each
day, pediatricians listen to bleary-eyed parents ask for help
because their child "isn't sleeping well." It's one of the most
common complaints pediatricians hear from the parents of
infants.

But if you listen carefully to what the parents are saying,
the baby's sleep isn't the real problem. Odds are, he's sleeping just fine. The baby's difficulty lies in how he goes to sleep
or wakes up—the transition to or from sleep. It's the *parents*

[1]Haim G. Ginott, *Between Parent & Child* (New York: Avon, 1969),
pp. 136–37.

who aren't sleeping well. Unlike your baby, you usually don't get to nap during the day.

We imbue sleep with values and symbols that extend far beyond its biological function. We picture the child who peacefully drifts off to sleep as having had a day well spent. We feel we have done a good job as parents. Unfortunately, this is nonsense. It also leads to parents incorrectly believing that if their baby isn't "sleeping well," they must be doing something wrong.

It takes up to several months for many babies to organize their sleep schedules into predictable patterns. This delay seems to reflect the immaturity of their nervous system. (A small proportion of babies sleep through the night—or at least don't wake their parents up during the night—from the very beginning. When our son was a newborn and waking us up three or four times a night, I grew to hate it when another parent casually mentioned that little Sam or Susie slept like a proverbial log. I wondered if this parent was making it up just so I'd feel even more tired during the day.)

Another reason new parents pay so much attention to sleep is that it's the primary occupation of newborn babies. For the first few weeks, much of their remaining time is spent eating, feeling drowsy, or feeling irritable. A typical newborn is only alert and active for several minutes of every hour she's awake.

THE ART AND SKILL OF
FALLING ASLEEP

Many babies have difficulty with the transition from wakefulness to sleep. Depending upon their temperament, some have more trouble than others. It's important to remember that even though we adults no longer give it a second thought, falling asleep by yourself is a skill that babies have to learn.

Developing a bedtime ritual from the very beginning is one simple way to help your baby master that skill. A bedtime ritual should be calming and simple. It's much harder for a baby to fall asleep if you've just tickled him or played with him. Try to do those things earlier in the evening and not just before your baby takes an afternoon nap. Instead, try more soothing activities like reading a story to him or listening to some quiet music. Some children find a warm bath relaxing, while others have so much fun in the tub that they're all wound up.

Sometimes your own behaviors inadvertently contribute to the problem. Until they're about eight weeks old, many babies fall asleep in their parents' arms while they're nursing or taking a bottle. The parent will then gently move the sleeping infant to his crib.

The problem occurs several hours later when the child wakes up and isn't sure how to get back to sleep again. So he cries. The mother comes in and holds and rocks the baby until he falls asleep in her arms. She then gently puts him back in his crib. Two hours later the baby wakes up again, has the same concern, and cries again. This time the father comes in and rocks him until he falls asleep. And so the cycle repeats, hour after hour, night after night, with both parents totally exhausted after only a few days of this.

Your apparent kindness is backfiring; your baby isn't learning how to fall asleep by himself. He's learning to become more dependent on you. Keep in mind that you don't really care if your baby wakes up several times during the night, as long as he can quickly fall back asleep without waking *you* up.

The solution is simple: Vary where and how your baby falls asleep. Sometimes let him fall asleep in your arms. (After all, it feels great.) But other times, as soon as you see his eyelids drooping, bring him to his crib. That way he'll be awake, but tired—and he'll make the transition to sleep by himself. And when he wakes up a few hours later, he'll remember what he did before and, more likely than not, will go back to sleep without waking you up.

Also remember that there are four stages of sleep. Your baby will be going from light sleep through the intermediate stages to deep sleep and then back up again several times during the night. These cycles usually take between three and four hours.

That means that every few hours your baby will probably stir, make noises, and even cry out, even though she's still in this lightest stage of sleep. For parents who are sensitive to those sounds, and for those who are using an electronic baby monitor or other intercom system, these normal noises may sound like your baby is crying for you.

So you rush in, ready to help. But remember, even though she's moving and making noise, odds are that your baby's still asleep. All you'll do if you try to "help" by taking her in your arms and soothing her is wake her up. In fact, if you look closely, you'll probably notice that your baby's trying to find her thumb or to get into the particular position that she finds most comfortable for making the transition to deeper sleep.

A good way to handle this is to wait two or three minutes before responding to those plaintive whimpers. That way, you can see if your baby settles down by herself. If she doesn't, then quietly go into her room. If her eyes are shut but she's softly crying, help her "find" her thumb. (I recommend that you use a thumb to help newborn babies because, unlike a security blanket or a pacifier, it's always in the same place. She can always find it when she needs it.[2])

Gently place it in her mouth. She'll begin sucking it, which will almost always stop the crying within seconds. Then you can watch as she quickly drifts into a deeper sleep. Remember that you're doing this to teach her a very important skill— how to quiet herself down when she's in distress. You may have to help her find her thumb a few more times, but she'll soon be able to do it by herself while she's asleep, and won't disturb you nearly as often.

---

[2]Note that there's a big difference between a baby who occasionally sucks her thumb for comfort and one whose thumb is in her mouth all the time. Occasional thumb sucking is a very effective stress reliever for a newborn. She should have little or no difficulty stopping later on, as long as she's learned other ways of handling stress. But a baby who's constantly sucking her thumb is probably bored and using it for stimulation rather than comfort. The way to handle that problem is to spend more time carrying, rocking, and playing with your baby.

There are two other things to keep in mind if your baby keeps waking you up during the night. Is his room too light? Some parents leave several night-lights on in their baby's room, which makes it more difficult for the child to discriminate between night (time for a long sleep) and day (time for a short nap). As one child psychologist friend of mine explains it with tongue in cheek, your baby only needs a lot of light at night if he's reading or he's entertaining guests.

Finally, remember that in your child's eyes, spending time with you is a tremendous amount of fun. It's very stimulating to have you pick him up, pat him, and talk to him. If he wakes up at three A.M. and is facing a choice between having fun and going back to sleep, he may choose to get you up, too.

When your baby wakes you up at night for reasons other than needing to be fed or changed, try to make your interaction as brief and unstimulating as possible. In essence, try to be boring to your baby when it's dark outside. Don't pick him up. Don't talk to him. Just get him back into a comfortable position, and leave.

This may sound heartless, but it's the best way of getting your child to recognize the difference between the behaviors you expect during the day, and those you want at night. Besides, you'll be a much better parent when you get your rest, too.

◆   ◆   ◆

TIPS FOR SLEEP PROBLEMS
AFTER A COLD

It feels like a great relief when your baby starts to sleep through the night, or at least stops waking you up. But you should expect some backsliding in certain situations.

One of the most common is after an illness. Even babies who have mild colds make their parents nervous and more protective. During the illness, your baby may have gotten used to your coming in once or twice during the night, especially if she's crying or needs some medicine. Being a good parent, you've comforted her and talked to her.

She knows a good thing when she sees it, of course. So when the cold is over and she wakes up during the night, she'll cry out for you. There's nothing malicious about this. In fact, you might even interpret it as a sign of intelligence. But it's a sign you probably don't want to see at three A.M.

Again, be the most boring parent you can during those hours of darkness. Don't talk to her except to say, "Go to sleep." Don't pick her up. Don't cuddle her. (If you're feeling guilty about this, you can promise yourself that you'll do some extra cuddling during the daytime.) If she's sitting or standing, just lay her down in her favorite sleeping position and leave the room.

Sometimes even this doesn't work. Your child may be especially tenacious in her demands for your attention. (Remember that this may work out for the best in the long run. Think about what a great salesperson she'll be, and how she'll buy you that retirement condo in Hawaii with all the money she'll make.) If this behavior happens, you'll need to take more dramatic and, for some parents, emotionally painful action.

Let your baby cry. I know this sounds terrible, and appears to fly in the face of what I wrote about the Cry-It-Out Myth earlier. But there's good reason to do it when four specific conditions are met:

♦ You know your baby is safe and isn't crying from pain. You've probably already checked to see if she looks sick or is running a fever. Your experience tells you that she simply wants attention.

♦ You have tried being as boring to your baby as possible during the night. You've done all the things I've described above to encourage her to go back to sleep.

♦ You have, in the past, regularly responded to your baby's cries by paying attention to her. This is critical. If your child has learned that you usually respond quickly to her cries, she'll get very frustrated when you don't, but will quickly stop trying when she doesn't get what she wants. But if you've been unpredictable and have come only a small percentage of the times when she's cried, she'll keep crying for longer periods. She's learned that being persistent sometimes pays off. (Remember those slot machines in Chapter 7!)

If you've been very inconsistent in the past, you're going to have a much tougher time with this. You may need to become more predictable during the daytime before you're bothered less at night. Even so, you should give this a try. After all, you're not sleeping anyway.

♦ She's lying down. If she's not, you may have to help her get horizontal again. Remember, some babies who've just learned to stand by holding on to the bars of their crib may go through a brief period when they'll stand there with their knees locked as if they can't remember how to sit down. In fact, that's precisely the problem, which is why they'll stand there and cry in frustration.

You can often help these children by gently nudging them from a standing position to a sitting position a few times. They'll find this delightful, and will giggle with glee. But you shouldn't be doing this at three A.M. Try it after an afternoon nap.

If all four of these are true, and you do it properly, not responding to her crying is a quick and extremely effective solution to the problem. If all four are not true, then ignoring her cries probably won't work, and isn't a good idea.

Let's say that your six-month-old daughter regularly slept through the night until a week ago when she had a cold. Her stuffy nose interfered with her breathing at night, so she would wake up and cry once or twice a night. Each time she cried, you went to her room, comforted her, gave her a decongestant, and sang her a lullaby as she drifted back to sleep. In effect, you were a warm, loving, patient, wonderful parent.

But now the cold is over, and your daughter still wakes up and cries for you. You've tried the "boring" routine, but to no avail. This time, as soon as she starts crying, stay in bed but look at a clock. This is important. We all have a distorted sense of time at night. It gets even more distorted if we're listening to something we find bothersome. If you didn't check a clock, you wouldn't know that the crying that felt like it lasted two hours actually only went on for fifteen minutes.

Don't try to ignore it and go to sleep. If you could do that, odds are you wouldn't have woken up in the first place. Thousands of years of genetics have made your baby's cry as compelling and attention-getting as it is. Instead, think about how much more relaxed and loving both you and your baby will be once you've both gotten enough sleep.

Once you've made a commitment to yourself not to go into your baby's room, stick with it. If you're really concerned, take a quick look at her every fifteen or twenty minutes to make sure she's not hurt, but try to go in and out silently and paying as little attention to her as possible. Remember how smart your baby is. If you go in after she's cried for twenty minutes and make a fuss over her, she'll learn that she shouldn't give up on you, and should cry for at least that long—which is the opposite of your goal.

I had to do this once with my son when he was about nine months old and was recovering from the croup. Even though I knew this would work, I put it off out of feelings of guilt and anxiety. What if he really needed me? What if he was sick again and I didn't know it? That wasn't the case, of course.

Finally, I braced myself to do what I had been telling other parents to do for years. He cried. I looked at the clock. It was 2:15 A.M. I braced myself. He cried louder. I buried my head in the pillow. He cried even louder and more plaintively. I felt miserable. This felt like it was going on forever. How could I do this to my own son? Finally his crying subsided and I could hear him gently snoring. With great trepidation I glanced at the clock to see how long our ordeal had lasted. It was 2:25 A.M.

The next night he slept without making a peep.

◆   ◆   ◆

INSIDE THE BRAIN OF A
SLEEPING BABY

One of the great mysteries of life is how newborn babies, who spend the vast majority of their time asleep or drowsy, can learn so many things so quickly. As adults, we associate learning with being awake and alert (despite what the advertisements for "sleep learning" tapes claim). We can see clues to what might be going on by closely observing sleeping babies, and keeping track of what their bodies and brains are doing. These clues have led some researchers to believe that newborn babies may be learning while they're asleep.

If you look closely at a sleeping newborn, you'll see that she often looks different from a sleeping adult. While she's in what scientists call "active sleep," her eyelids may be partly open, allowing you to see the pupils moving slowly and regularly, or in rapid, jerky motions. Her muscles may twitch and spasm. She may try to toss her head backward and to the side, then quickly try to turn her torso in the same direction—an attempt at acrobatics that, while she was in the womb only a few days earlier, would have caused her to rotate to a new and, perhaps, more comfortable position. During "quiet sleep" she appears more peaceful. Even so, her entire body may seem to spasm at the same time. Her heart may race and her breathing become irregular.

Even when your child may seem to be resting peacefully and snoring lightly, her brain is working at a furious pace. Millions of brain cells are "firing"—showing electrical activity—every second, generating a strong-enough signal to be measured by electrodes placed on the surface of her head. The graphs of these brain-cell activities, known as electroencephalograms or EEGs, look like sketches of city skylines or mountain ranges, with electrical peaks occurring several times each second.

While adult EEGs show a marked decrease in activity during sleep, newborn EEGs do not. If you flash a light or make a clicking noise at a sleeping adult and look at the EEG, you won't see much of a reaction, compared to the reaction you'd get if that adult were awake. But if you do the same thing to a newborn, you'll get almost exactly the same brain-wave response whether the baby's awake or asleep. It's almost as if, while her body's asleep, her brain is awake.

By the time your baby is three months old, she's probably sleeping through much of the night. Her EEG pattern has changed as well, and is looking more like an adult's. This special period appears to be over.

CHAPTER 11

Food for Thought

When I was a year old I stopped eating everything except bread
and milk. . . . I come from a long line of people with unusual
food preferences.
—ALEXANDRA W. LOGUE, PH.D.[1]

Eating is the other problem you're very likely to discuss
with your pediatrician. We associate food with deep cultural
meanings that go well beyond its nutritional value. Food is a
source of reassurance ("comfort foods") and a sign of friend-
ship and respect (to "break bread" with someone). It is present at our celebrations. (What birthday or wedding would be
complete without cake?) It is a sign of wealth and power. (A
person who serves you champagne and caviar is sending a
very strong message that has little to do with grapes and
fish eggs.) It's no coincidence that when Norman Rockwell
wanted to show the archetype of the American family gather-
ing, he painted three generations sitting down to an abundant
Thanksgiving dinner.

We interpret how well our children eat as a measure of
how well we are doing during our first few weeks as parents.
But often, this interpretation is wrong. It also induces unnec-

[1]A. W. Logue, *The Psychology of Eating and Drinking*, (New York: W. H.
Freeman, 1991) p. ix.

essary guilt in parents who, by all other measures, are doing just fine.

BREAST-FEEDING VERSUS BOTTLE-FEEDING

Here's an issue that's sure to raise the ire of those who are committed to either position. I've enjoyed the impassioned debate, largely because I'm thrilled to see people on both sides who are so committed to their children's nutrition. I become concerned, however, when parents are made to feel like failures if they do not follow a particular approach.

Both sides have been guilty of such cruel propaganda. Adamant breast milk advocates have warned (inaccurately) that bottle-fed babies do not emotionally bond to their mothers as well. (This has been especially painful to adoptive mothers and others who, for biological reasons, cannot nurse their babies.) Infant formula manufacturers have told mothers in third-world countries that breast milk wasn't as good for their babies as their commercial product—which is also a lie. In fact, this led to cases of infant malnutrition and diarrhea, as poor parents, who used their meager funds to buy the unneeded formula to help their babies, prepared it in unsanitary conditions and with contaminated water.

So let's put the emotions of breast-feeding versus bottle-feeding aside for a few pages and deal with the facts. First, with today's commercial formulas for newborns, you don't have to feel that you're depriving your baby of any necessary nutrients. (Note that feeding your child cow's milk is not an adequate substitute for human milk or formula.) An average bottle-fed baby will thrive as well as a breast-fed baby.[2] So

[2]There's one small study published in Great Britain involving high-risk infants that found that babies who were given breast milk or a combination of breast milk and formula appeared to have higher IQs a few years later than those who were given only formula. That report got a good bit of publicity. But it's unclear whether that difference in IQ was really due to

adequate nutrition—the biggest concern—shouldn't be an issue.

Each approach has advantages and disadvantages. If the mother is well-fed, breast milk is an ideal diet for a newborn. It has all a baby needs for growth during the first few months of life, with the possible exception of fluoride and Vitamin D, which are easily given as supplements. Talk to your pediatrician about that.

Breast-feeding has some biochemical advantages as well. Even though your baby may be nursing soon after birth, he's not getting any of your milk, which won't be produced by your body until about the third day. Instead, you're feeding him a yellowish liquid known as colostrum, which seems to transfer some of your own disease-preventing antibodies to him. This may protect him against certain viruses.

Also, a breast-feeding mother doesn't have to be worried about her baby being allergic to her milk. Breast milk is sterile, readily available (to the mother, at least), and you never have to worry about its temperature. It can also be manually expressed and refrigerated, so that it's available when the mother isn't around.

Although many (but not all) babies will try to nurse immediately after birth, their efforts meet with varying success. Extracting milk from a breast takes a bit of coordination. Bottles present less of a problem that way. An experienced nurse will be able to show you some tips to help your baby get the hang of it without becoming too frustrated. Don't be surprised if it takes him a few tries to become a successful breast-feeder.

You may also find that your baby has trouble "disconnecting" from your breast when he's through or when you

the food or might be attributable, for instance, to a combination of the health of the babies at birth, the amount of stimulation they got from their parents, and chance. Keep in mind, when you read about studies like this, that lots of formula-fed babies, just like breast-fed babies, develop extremely high intelligence, so it doesn't look like either method puts a "ceiling" on how smart your child can be.

want to switch him to the other side. If you simply pull him off you'll not only frustrate him, you'll find it rather painful. Instead, gently insert a finger between his lips and your breast to break the vacuum.

Many women find breast-feeding a warm, soothing, or even erotic experience. It is a special time for them to feel close to their babies and revel in their new relationship. Others find it a frustrating, exhausting, and occasionally painful process. As the weeks go on, they find themselves resenting the constant demands from their babies and the changes in their bodies. They may need to return to work within several weeks following their delivery, and may not have a place to express and store their milk during the day.

There are numerous books to help mothers cope with these problems. *The most important thing to remember is that deciding not to breast-feed your baby, or being unable to do so, does not make you a bad parent.* In fact, worrying too much about your decision is much more likely to lead to problems, because you'll feel unnecessarily guilty and anxious. Also remember that it's your body, so it's your choice. Don't feel pressured or bullied by anyone, including your spouse, parents or physician, or a formula manufacturer.

There are advantages and disadvantages to bottle-feeding as well. (That's actually a misnomer, since parents who express breast milk also use bottles.) Commercial formula is one of the great equalizers—fathers can give it to their babies as easily as mothers can. So can grandparents, baby-sitters, and others who want to get in on the act.

One of the advantages of bottle-feeding is that it allows fathers to spend more time caring for their baby. This isn't just a matter of family efficiency or fairness. The time spent feeding a baby, like the time spent with the mother during prenatal checkups and labor and delivery, allows fathers to feel more like an integral and needed part of their child's life from the very beginning. That not only helps the father-child relationship, it can prevent feelings of jealousy and resentment as well.

Many first-time parents who use a formula choose the

brand that they saw being used in their hospital. They interpret its selection of that particular brand as a tacit endorsement of the product's superior quality. After all, how many television commercials for pain relievers have you seen that say something like, "The brand hospitals use the most"?

Bear in mind that formula makers, like pain-reliever and disposable-diaper manufacturers, are acutely aware of this tendency, and will offer hospitals extremely low prices in the hope that parents will stick with the same brand over the coming months. So don't feel that you have to use the same brand of formula or diapers or anything else your hospital used. The fact that they selected those brands doesn't mean they're necessarily better for your baby. More likely, it's a testament to the skill and savvy of the manufacturers' marketing departments.

◆   ◆   ◆

TIPS FOR USING COMMERCIAL INFANT FORMULA

Commercial infant formula comes in three forms, with price being proportional to convenience. At the top of the line are single-serving, vacuum-packed, ready-to-eat bottles of formula which, if purchased at a drug or convenience store, can cost as much per ounce as a fairly good bottle of wine. The advantage of these is that you can simply screw a retaining ring and nipple onto the jar, and have an instant, sterile bottle. They're great for emergencies and for traveling, since you don't have to worry about refrigeration.

Larger containers of ready-to-serve or concentrated formula are much more reasonably priced, and will allow you to make a day's worth of bottles at a time. If you're making formula from a powder—which is the least expensive way to purchase it—it takes a bit of work to do it right. (Remember those cases of diarrhea in third-world countries? It can happen in your kitchen, too.)

You'll have to make an effort to see that the utensils,

bottles, and nipples you're using are very clean. This doesn't mean you have to put on a surgical scrub suit and boil everything in sight. But you should use a bottle brush to wash the bottles and nipples with hot soapy water. If you leave the measuring scoop or spoon in the container of powdered formula, be sure to wash your hands well before you touch it so you don't inadvertently contaminate the formula. If you leave it outside the container, wash the scoop with hot, soapy water before you use it each time.

It sounds trite, but be sure to follow the manufacturer's directions for making the formula. Also, don't attempt to "supercharge" the formula by not diluting it as much as the directions say. Babies' kidneys have trouble handling formula that's too concentrated.

Much has been made of the proper temperature at which to serve formula. With breast-feeding, this is never a problem, of course. But parents who bottle-feed their children will sometimes go through elaborate rituals of heating the formula in a pan of hot water or an electric bottle warmer, then squirting a few drops onto the inside of their wrists or elbows to check the temperature. While this may seem easy at two o'clock in the afternoon, it feels considerably more complicated and seems to take much longer at four o'clock in the morning.

My experience with this, as well as that of the pediatricians I've spoken with about it, is that many children really don't care whether their formula or expressed breast milk is warm or cold. (My own son seemed to prefer it straight from the refrigerator when he was an infant.)

What you don't want is for the formula to be hot—which is a risk you take whenever you warm up a bottle. That's also why you should never use a microwave oven to warm up a baby's bottle. Even though the drop or two you test can feel cool, part of the formula can be extremely hot and can scald your baby's mouth.

Finally, if your baby seems to be having difficulty digesting a particular formula (for example, he spits up large amounts of it, develops diarrhea, or becomes gassy), don't worry that it's because you're doing something wrong or because your child is angry at you. Talk with your pediatrician. You may be able to solve the problem quickly by switching to a soy-based formula.

◆   ◆   ◆

THE EMOTIONS OF FOOD

One woman I interviewed was noticeably upset as she described her infant son. He had rejected breast-feeding—something she had eagerly looked forward to—in favor of formula. She described his eating as a "feeding frenzy" that was so intense the boy broke out in a sweat whenever he had a bottle.

Objectively, the child was doing well. He was gaining weight and obviously thriving. But his style of eating wasn't as she had anticipated, and was, in fact, quite different from his older sister's when she was a newborn. The boy's rejection of his mother's breast had led her to question her fundamental competence as a parent, even though she'd done well with her daughter and, by any objective measure, was doing just fine with her son as well.

It was a good demonstration of the powerful emotions we associate with eating. If her baby had rejected a particular rattle or chosen a different sleeping pattern from his sister's, this mother wouldn't have been nearly as upset. But because her son's action had involved food, and especially breast-feeding, she interpreted it as a rejection of their overall relationship.

Many of the feeding problems that parents of newborns have described to me come from their not being sensitive to their baby's communications about eating. These parents try to impose their own preconceived notions or rigid schedules on their baby's developing digestive system. Instead of better nutrition, they wind up with more frustration, a fussier baby, and larger cleaning bills.

Almost all babies are good at controlling when and how much they eat so that they get enough nourishment. But that doesn't mean that you should feed your baby every time he makes a noise. He'll quickly adapt to going for a few hours without food, especially if he can find some other source of comfort, such as a baby blanket, a stuffed animal, a pacifier, or you.

Remember that your baby will probably have a very disorganized and unpredictable eating-sleeping-activity pattern during the first few weeks after his birth. You'll find that frustrating and exhausting, especially since you may not be able to get more than a few hours of sleep at a time. Soon, however, your baby will develop more of a regular rhythm to her daily routine, and the periods of each activity will grow longer.

If you try to force a baby to eat when she's no longer hungry, she'll probably become upset and quickly deposit the extra food on either her shirt or yours. Similarly, if you try to take her away from her food while she's still eating because you think she's had enough or needs to be burped, she'll become upset and may cry, spit up food, or both. Some parents unconsciously jiggle or bounce their babies while feeding them—an approach that would make dining a particularly unpleasant experience for anyone.

The key is to become sensitive to the messages your baby is sending you while she eats. Many of these messages are subtle. Look for a pattern. Your baby may stop sucking when she wants a minute's rest, but turn her face away a bit when she's had enough to eat. Also remember that babies like sucking for comfort as well as food. If your baby is eating only a very small amount each time, you may be misinterpreting her need for comfort as hunger.

Parents in this situation usually complain that their babies always act like they're hungry, but don't seem to eat very much. If that's the case, you might want to try substituting a pacifier for a bottle or breast some of the times that your baby seems to want food. You may find that he's just as happy. And because he's not eating as often, he'll eat more when he has a meal.

One other thing that can help avoid feeding problems in newborns is to help your baby focus on the task at hand. Eating takes a bit of coordination. If your baby is drowsy or distracted, she's going to have more difficulty eating. Try talking to her gently for a minute before you feed her. Often this simple act will increase her level of attention so that she's more coordinated and a better eater.

THE TRANSITION TO SOLID FOOD

Eating solids is seen as a sign of maturity. While many cultures breast-feed for several years, thereby guaranteeing better nutrition for children than might otherwise be available, Americans often take great pride in how quickly their children stop. This reached an epitome of silliness a few years ago when parents were encouraged to give their children solid foods during the first two or three weeks of life, in the belief that they would sleep longer during the night. (In reality, children's sleep patterns tend to reflect how mature their nervous systems are, not what they've recently eaten.)

While digesting some of these foods might not be a problem for newborns, swallowing them is. Swallowing a solid food takes much more muscular coordination than sucking a liquid. Newborns simply haven't wired those particular circuits in their brains yet. If the solid food (usually a cereal of some sort) was diluted and held on a spoon near the baby's lips, he could probably suck it down as if it were milk or formula. But all too often, parents simply dumped a small spoonful on the back of their infant's tongue, causing him to gag and spit it out. It also made him less interested in trying any more.

Giving your baby solid foods before he can reliably swallow them will probably frustrate and anger both of you. Just remember that your baby is still getting adequate nutrition without them, and that he'll master the coordination he needs at about the same age, whether you give him solid foods early or not. If you wait until he's five or six months old, he'll probably successfully swallow his first spoonful of food without any fuss.

◆   ◆   ◆

FUSSY EATERS

Combinations of four factors seem to influence whether your baby will act like a fussy eater at any given time: temperament, biochemistry, environment, and development. As I mentioned in Chapter 8, some babies seem to have much lower sensory thresholds than others. One of those senses is taste. Just as some babies are more bothered by bright lights or loud sounds, others appear to be more sensitive to either particular foods or any new food. This can be a particular problem for newborns since, when you're being breast- or bottle-fed, *every-thing* else is a new food.

These taste-sensitive and texture-sensitive children are also more likely to have difficulty settling into a daily routine over the first few months, thereby making any eating problem seem more dramatic. For them, new foods are best introduced in small quantities and in familiar surroundings. Your baby's more likely to swallow a new type of cereal at home than at a neighbor's house.

Biochemistry and development also play roles in how babies taste food and what tastes they prefer at different ages. According to Dr. Gary Beauchamp, who studies smell and taste as a researcher at the Monell Chemical Senses Center at the University of Pennsylvania, children are born with a preference for sweet tastes, but have little interest in salt. By the time they're four months old, however, babies will prefer to drink a mild salt solution to plain water.

Also, he's found that young children appear to be especially finicky about food that tastes bitter. That aversion may be one of the reasons our ancestors survived, since many poisonous plants have a bitter taste.

Some children can taste chemicals in food that others cannot. One example of this is the chemical with the tongue-twisting name *phenylthiocarbamide,* also known as PTC. It's present in a number of bitter-tasting green vegetables such as kale. Studies have shown that some people are very sensitive to tiny amounts of PTC in a food, while others require a much larger amount of the chemical to taste it at all.

According to Dr. Linda Bartoshuk of Yale University, who has studied taste, about two thirds of Americans can taste PTC in small concentrations. The differences in sensitivity appear to come from our genes.

Your baby's stage of development also plays a role in how fussy he is at mealtime. Holding a bottle and picking up a piece of food with fingers or a spoon are skills that babies are rightfully proud of. (So are blowing bubbles and spitting food, for that matter, although parents tend to be less appreciative of those particular accomplishments.)

You can expect your baby to act differently at mealtimes as he's trying to master such new skills. Simply picking up food, for example, may appear to be more important to him than getting it in his mouth. Dropping a spoon on the floor can turn into a great game for a baby when he realizes that every time he does it, his mother or father picks it up.

It's important to allow a child at this stage to have increasing responsibility for feeding himself, even though he's guaranteed to make quite a mess of it. The old warning, "Don't play with your food!" simply doesn't apply to babies. It's through playing with their food that they master the skills they need to eat well.

This is where environmental factors enter into eating problems. No amount of lecturing will convince an eleven-month-old not to spill his cup of juice. After all, he's learning so much and having a great deal of fun seeing what happens when he holds it upside down!

Instead, look for ways to minimize damage rather than

trying to eliminate the behavior. Use unbreakable plastic cups with lids that have spouts. Only put a small amount of liquid in the cup at a time. Put newspapers or a drop-cloth under his high chair. (A friend of mine recommends getting a large dog who will happily slurp up any scraps of food that fall to the ground.)

If you do these things, and your child throws the cup on the floor and the lid pops off, you'll only have to deal with an ounce or two of liquid. You might also want to try plates and bowls that have suction cups on their bottoms to adhere to the high chair's tray and prevent a mass dumping of food. Or you forgo plates completely for a while, and put your baby's food directly on the tray.

Finally, don't get into a battle with your child over food. You're sure to lose it. Mealtime is one of the best ways for developing babies to test the amount of power and control they have in their lives. The issue driving an apparently fussy eater may have little to do with the food itself. The more you try to force a particular food on him, the more he'll clench his teeth and refuse to eat it.

Instead, relax. Back off. Remember that skipping a meal or two won't hurt him. Give him the control he's looking for—which can be as simple as letting him hold the spoon or eat at his own rate. He'll become more cooperative, and you'll both have more enjoyable meal-times.

◆   ◆   ◆

CHAPTER 12

The Trouble with Expert Advice

I have wanted babies for years and now I am so tired and with the unfinished work everyday and everywhere I turn, I could scream at their constant prattle.
—FROM A LETTER WRITTEN IN 1920 TO JULIA LATHROP, DIRECTOR OF THE CHILDREN'S BUREAU[1]

It may appear self-defeating to write a chapter with a title like this. My goal is not to have you shun all expert advice. Rather, I hope you'll remember to trust your instincts, experiences, and common sense when you read and listen to the many people, child development professionals and others, who will try to tell you how to be a better parent. You can learn a great deal from other people's research, training, and experience, of course. But it's sometimes more important to know when you shouldn't pay attention to what they're saying.

Parents, especially new parents, are emotionally vulnerable. We each want to provide our children with the best. Given the choice between buying what we perceive as a pretty

[1] As quoted in M. Konner, *Childhood* (Boston: Little, Brown, 1991), p. 107.

good toy or outfit and a better one for a few dollars more, we'll usually spend the extra money. (Sometimes this is taken to extremes. After all, how many babies really care if they're wearing designer clothes that cost as much as most people earn in a week?)

These noble desires make parents fair game for people who can exploit our feelings of uncertainty and our desires to provide the best for our children. Sometimes this exploitation is intentional and unscrupulous. Other times it's done with the best of intentions. In either case, it's important to feel confident in making your own decisions, even if they result in mistakes and missed opportunities. No one's a perfect parent.

The emotional plea for help at the beginning of this chapter was written by an overwhelmed mother three quarters of a century ago. But her desire to do her work well, her good intentions and best wishes for her children, as well as her frustration over their constant demands, are the same words we hear from today's worried parents. Among the likely contributors to the intensity of her emotions—and often making her feel worse as well as better—were changes during her generation in the science of developmental psychology and in the role of government in family life. Allow me to take a few pages to provide a quick and very sketchy history lesson that will show how our culture sometimes encourages us to feel unnecessarily guilty, angry, and incompetent as parents.

THE SCIENCE OF GUILT

Parenting was seen as a "science" for the first time during the late 1800s and early 1900s. The advice given to parents was filled with schedules and proscriptions—an overwhelming collection of rigid rules. People like John B. Watson,[2] the

[2]If you've taken a course in introductory psychology and are having trouble placing this name, it may help to recall that Watson was the man who got a happy and healthy eleven-month-old baby, known as Little Albert, to develop a fear of rabbits, rats, and other furry items. When Albert was first introduced to a harmless (and cute) laboratory rat, he reached out

founder of behaviorism, claimed that family and school environments were all-important in a child's development—thereby increasing the amount of guilt parents felt if they didn't do everything absolutely "right."

Today's introductory psychology and child development texts love to quote Watson's writings as reflections of those times. For example:

> Treat [children] as though they were young adults. Dress them, bathe them with care and circumspection.[3] Let your behavior always be objective and kindly firm. Never hug and kiss them, never let them sit in your lap. If you must, kiss them once on the forehead when they say good night. Shake hands with them in the morning. Give them a pat on the head if they have made an extraordinarily good job of a difficult task. Try it out. In a week's time you will find how easy it is to be perfectly objective with your child and at the same time kindly. You will be utterly ashamed of the mawkish, sentimental way you have been handling it. . . .
>
> Remember when you are tempted to pet your child that mother love is a dangerous . . . instrument which may inflict

to pet it without hesitation. As he did so, Watson made a loud noise with an iron bar that he held behind the baby's head, causing Albert to startle and jerk back his hand. Watson did this a few times, until it became clear that Albert didn't want to be near the rat.

A week later, when Watson brought the baby back into his laboratory and showed him the rat—but didn't strike the iron bar to make a loud noise—Little Albert crawled away so quickly he almost fell off the table where he'd been placed. The baby had developed an acute fear, or phobia, of rats. Several weeks after the initial pairing of the rat and the loud noise, Albert showed the same fear of not only the rat, but also became upset when he saw a rabbit, a dog, his mother's fur coat, and even a mask of Santa Claus that had a furry, white beard.

While Watson's experiments with Little Albert have contributed a great deal to our understanding of the development of certain phobias and the appropriate treatments for them, Albert's parents apparently had second thoughts about what was happening to their son. They stopped taking him to Watson's laboratory. To this day, we don't know if Albert spent the rest of his life wondering why Christmas and fur coats made him so anxious.

[3] One of the reasons I've loved this absurd quote since I first read it in college is that I've never been able to figure out how you actually bathe a child with circumspection!

a never healing wound, a wound which may make infancy unhappy, adolescence a nightmare, an instrument which may wreck your adult son or daughter's vocational future and their chances for marital happiness.[4]

Never hug and kiss your children! Mother love may make your children's infancy unhappy and prevent them from pursuing a career or getting married! That's total hogwash, of course. But it shows an extreme example of what state-of-the-art "scientific" parenting was supposed to be in early twentieth-century America. After all, that was the heyday of efficiency experts, time-and-motion studies, and the like.

Watson, who eventually left academic psychology to pursue a very successful career in advertising, viewed parents largely as a source of damage to their children. Instead of traditional homes, he envisioned "baby farms" where hundreds of infants would be raised and scientifically observed.

In his ideal world, child rearing would be brought as much as possible under laboratory control. Mothers would not know the identity of their children. Breast feeding would be prohibited, and children would be rotated among families at four-week intervals until the age of twenty.[5]

Declarations like Watson's put parents in emotional quicksand. No matter what they did, it was wrong—and it dragged them deeper into an abyss of self-blame and unwarranted guilt. (The competing psychological theory of the day, promoted by Sigmund Freud and his followers, was pretty good at inducing parental guilt as well!)

The federal government encouraged this through some of the publications of The Children's Bureau, a branch of the Department of Labor that was founded in 1912 after a six-

[4]J. B. Watson, *Psychological Care of Infant and Child* (New York: Norton, 1928), pp. 81–87.

[5]K. W. Buckley, *Mechanical Man: John Broadus Watson and the Beginnings of Behaviorism* (New York: Guilford, 1989), p. 163.

year battle in Congress. The Children's Bureau was mandated
to "investigate and report . . . upon all matters pertaining to
the welfare of children and child life among all classes of our
people. . . ."[6]

It was a highly innovative program that studied the causes
and prevention of infant mortality, enforced the first federal
child-labor law, studied the effects on children of their mothers' employment outside the home during World War I, and
developed and administered a federal program for states that
provided aid to pregnant women and newborn babies. The
Children's Bureau also published countless reports, books,
and pamphlets with titles ranging from *Save 100,000 Babies,
Get a Square Deal for Children* to *Patriotic Play Week: Suggestions
to Local Committees.*

It also distributed what were known as "dodgers"—short,
instructional handbills on basic child-care topics like "What
Do Growing Children Need?" and "Feeding the Child."
Thus, the federal government endorsed "official" ways that
parents should act. Each year, the Bureau received tens of
thousands of letters from distraught parents asking for advice.

The official replies these parents received, and the pamphlets that accompanied them, emphasized the need for
rigid, efficient—but often impossible—schedules. The result
was not only predictable tension in the households, but parents who felt that they were incompetent because they
couldn't stick to what, on paper at least, looked so simple.

Although we can now look back on these well-intended
pieces of advice with amusement, they have not completely
left us. For example, I received a book in the mail the other
day that purported to help me teach my child to read. It was
written by a "reading consultant" and carried a pair of back-

[6]J. A. Tobey, *The Children's Bureau: Its History, Activities and Organization*
(Baltimore: Johns Hopkins Press, 1925). The first congressional appropria-
tion for this massive task was $25,640, which paid for a staff of fifteen
people. Within three years, The Children's Bureau staff had increased to
seventy-six and the annual budget had grown to $164,640.

cover endorsements (known in the trade as "blurbs") from professors at respected schools.

By chance, I opened it to a chapter titled "Please Don't Teach the ABCs," where I read the sentence "Personal experience has shown me repeatedly that knowing the alphabet names can be a handicap to children."

I was stunned. My son, who is two years old as I write this, has been singing the alphabet song for about nine months. He loves playing with plastic letters and takes great glee at identifying them by name. Clearly, my wife and I had a role in his learning this information. We realize that naming the letters is very different from learning to read.

But there I was, reading a book by a "reading consultant" who just informed me that by teaching our son the alphabet we had "handicapped" him. How was I supposed to feel? More important, what was I supposed to do? Perhaps we should take away all his letters, even though he revels in his mastery of their names. Maybe we should hide all printed material from him. How about changing what my wife and I call each letter so that our son stays confused for the next few years, in the hope that we can "un-handicap" him when he attends school?

I'm being facetious, of course. But this type of rigid, unrealistic message pervades much of the advice parents receive from experts. Rather than being helpful, these unsubstantiated, blanket statements simply make parents more upset and anxious.

The next time you hear a piece of advice like that, use a little common sense. Did you learn the letters of the alphabet before you learned how to read? (I did.) Can you read well? (I can.) The reading consultant's advice just doesn't make sense. Sure, there are some children who will have difficulty with the transition from knowing the name of the letter to knowing the sound it usually makes. But using that as a basis for prohibiting parents from having fun teaching their children the alphabet is not only nonsensical, it's cruel.

◆   ◆   ◆

BEWARE THE SUPERBABY
SYNDROME

Some unscrupulous people try to exploit the insecurities and desires parents naturally have. They'll promise to turn your child into a prodigy if you'll just buy their program or products and do exactly what they say.

There are lots of simple, inexpensive ways you can help your baby develop to his fullest potential. Read to him often and from an early age. Play with him. Encourage him to explore. Spend time cuddling.

Don't feel you have to buy special courses or lots of expensive toys. Instead, think of some toys you can make at home. (I've described several of these in Chapter 9.)

I've often thought that a great (but unethical) way to make a small fortune would be to publish a book of child development charts that were intentionally distorted, so that approximately 85 percent of children were shown to be "above average" or "ahead of schedule" in when they learned to sit up, talk, walk, pick up a block, etc. Like so many disreputable and worthless programs, it would succeed financially by appealing to parents' insecurity and vanity.

A child psychologist friend of mine and I once joked that we should write a tongue-in-cheek press release about a new prenatal education system. Our whimsical and totally fraudulent approach involved a high-intensity slide projector that aimed pictures of classical paintings and mathematical formulas onto a pregnant mother's belly. The slides would all be reversed and inverted, we noted, because they would be seen by the baby who was upside down and on the other side of the "screen."

It was our way of responding to some of the ludicrous claims made by people who take parents' money under the pretense of turning their babies into geniuses.[7] We

---

[7]The idea was inspired by a similarly tongue-in-cheek radio advertising campaign I'd heard that had been put together by

were particularly upset by the way some of these programs implied that if they didn't work, it was because
the parents had somehow failed.

The problem with our idea, we soon realized, was that
a significant number of people would take it seriously.
After all, one entrepreneur was offering escorted group
tours of the Orient for two-year-olds and their parents,
with the promise that the two weeks of such cross-cul-
tural exposure would help the children in kindergarten
and beyond!

Whenever you see an offer like this, keep in mind that
infants are already learning at an incredibly fast rate. We
don't have to encourage them to learn; they'll even do
that in spite of us if they have to. It's wired into their
genes. But infants learn in ways that reflect the stages of
development of their brains.

I recall one woman who, under social pressure from
her family and neighbors, enrolled her baby in an expensive art class that was, she soon discovered, completely
inappropriate to his stage of development. As she put it,
"When they took out the crayons, he ate the crayons.
When they took out the clay, he ate the clay."

Advertisements for many of these expensive, inappropriate, and generally worthless programs appeal to our
vanity as parents. At best, they do nothing to help our
children's intellects and talents. At worst, they add significantly to the stress children and parents feel, and may
actually lead to academic problems later on.

◆   ◆   ◆

a classical music station in Cleveland. One of their announcers
was apparently upset at the television commercials for "Great
Moments in Music" or some similar collection of brief excerpts
from symphonies and operas. He retaliated by broadcasting
some fake radio commercials for "Great Square Inches in Art."
Much to his surprise, he received quite a few orders, including
one from a local public school. One astute listener, however,
mailed in a square inch of a check.

BE SKEPTICAL ABOUT ENDORSEMENTS

One of the ways I, like many people, judge the quality of a product or service before buying it is by finding out what other people think about it. After all, that's why advertisers spend a fortune for celebrity endorsements. When it comes to products for children, however, I've recently become more skeptical. Here's one of the reasons:

About a year ago I was approached by a children's book club that wanted to put me on its Board of Advisers. Since I strongly believe in the importance of parents reading to their children, I asked them for more information. As we spoke, it became clear that they didn't really want my advice. They simply wanted my name on their letterhead to lend it greater credibility. They also asked for a copy of my signature so that they could affix it to letters they'd send to parents—without my having any control over the content of the letter. For this, they offered to pay me a thousand dollars per year.

I didn't know whether to feel more insulted that they thought I'd compromise my ethics at all, or that if I did, I'd do so for so little money! Needless to say, I promptly turned them down.

To this day, every so often I receive a manipulative, guilt-inducing form letter from this book club written by a skilled copywriter. The letter tells me how I will be doing my son a terrible disservice unless I not only read to him (they're right!), but buy their particular children's books (they're wrong!). It's signed by some psychologist, psychiatrist, or television star, and the "Board of Advisors" on the letterhead is filled with people whose names you know. I wonder how well they sleep at night.

◆   ◆   ◆

ONE PROGRAM THAT WORKS

Luckily, one of the best ways you can help your baby grow intellectually is also the least expensive and, perhaps, the easiest to do. Read to her. It doesn't have to be anything special because it's the act of reading aloud and the interaction with your child that's important, not the contents of the books. You can use library books as well as books and magazines you have around the house.

In the beginning, it really won't matter which books you read or how well you read them aloud. Try some poetry, some romance, an adventure story, or even a cookbook. Ask her what she thinks of the plot or whether she feels the recipe is interesting.

You won't get much of a response, of course. At least not in words. But if you look closely, you'll probably notice that you have her rapt attention. She'll watch your face and listen to the melody and rhythms of your voice. If she's fussy, it may help her calm down.

The point is to use this as a time to cuddle with your child, and have her associate time spent reading and listening as something pleasurable. Odds are, this association will stay with her during her toddler and preschool years, when the content of the stories begins to make a difference. (She'll be less interested in romance, and more interested in Dr. Seuss.)

You'll probably find that you get at least as much out of the reading as your baby will. It's a good change of pace—a time when the two of you can relax together and simply have some fun.

◆   ◆   ◆

CHAPTER 13

Support Systems

Before I married I had three theories about raising children.
Now I have three children and no theories
—JOHN WILMOT, EARL OF ROCHESTER (1647–1680)

You can't raise children alone. You can't even do it just as a couple. The task is too overwhelming. One of the most difficult challenges new parents face is arranging for support systems both for you and for your children.

It used to be a lot simpler, when several generations of a family shared both their home and their experience. "Day care" (which should really be called "child care") was unheard of. Preschool didn't exist. If you needed to take a break, a grandparent or other relative was around who could care for your child while you gathered your wits, did some work, or indulged in a much-needed nap.

But *simpler* doesn't necessarily mean *better*. Children can gain a great deal from some forms of child care that provide love, stimulation, and a chance to practice social skills. Parents who don't feel trapped by their babies tend to be more patient and loving. The problem lies in building a support system that meets your needs, your aspirations for yourself and your family, and your budget.

I emphasize "building a support system" because you'll need to combine several approaches to caring for your child.

I think of it as a system rather than a structure because you can expect to change your approaches during the first few years as your needs, your situation, and your baby change. First-time parents often begin by thinking of a single solution—"I'll care for my baby by myself at home" or "I'll use a family child-care provider when I'm at work." Those individual approaches work well as long as you never have any other problems. What if you or your child-care provider get sick? What if you have to work late? What if you need to be somewhere during the evening?

In Chapter 1, I advised you to make some decisions about child care before your child is born. This would include, of course, finding out your employer's policies regarding time off, benefits, how long your job will be held for you, etc. It's a good idea to make note of all these policies since, soon after your child's birth, you may change your original plans.

I've run across quite a few parents—both mothers and fathers—who were surprised at how different their feelings about raising their children were once those children came home. Their shifts in attitudes and desires went in either direction. Some were unexpectedly enthralled with the idea of spending as much time as possible with their children, and were trying to work part-time or leave their jobs so that they could become full-time parents. Others, who expected to devote several years to caring for their children full-time, discovered that they felt stifled and angry. Their resentment interfered with the idyllic relationship they had imagined. These parents felt they needed to go back to work quickly so that they could feel more comfortable and loving when they were with their children and their spouses.

For many parents, of course, going back to work soon after childbirth is not a matter of choice. It's a financial necessity. Even so, there are many ways of building a support system that will allow you and your children to benefit the most.

♦ ♦ ♦

ASSESSING YOUR CHILD-CARE NEEDS AND ATTITUDES

It's a good idea to do this both while you're pregnant (or even earlier!) and soon after you give birth. Caring for children always takes more time and effort than you anticipated. It's better to err on the side of thinking you have too much support, than assuming that you have enough.

Begin by asking yourself some questions, and talk over your answers with your spouse:

♦ What makes someone a good parent? (How, if at all, is that related to who provides child care during most of the day?)

♦ What do you think about your friends who choose to stay home full-time with their children? (Are you jealous? Do you think they're being stupid? Does it matter if they're men or women?)

♦ What do you think about your friends who choose to go back to work full-time soon after their children are born? (Are you jealous? Do you think they're being stupid? Does it matter if they're men or women?)

♦ How did your parents care for you when you were a child? (Do you wish it had been different? How is it a factor in your own choice? How were your mother's responsibilities different from your father's?)

♦ If you're planning on going back to work, when? (Fathers as well as mothers should answer this! Why did you choose that time period? What would happen if you returned to work earlier/later?)

♦ Who has primary responsibility at home for caring for your baby? (Don't say you'll share it evenly. Odds are you won't, at least in the short-term. Try to be specific about tasks, such as who'll do most of the feeding, changing, etc. Also, will there be a different distribution of responsibilities during the day than in the evening? What about weekends?)

♦ If your child is too sick to go to outside child care, and one of you has to stay home with him, which of you will it be? (How will you decide? What other people might help you out on short notice?)

♦ How will you handle the anger and frustration you're sure to feel as a new parent, without taking it out on your baby? (Will you need quiet time alone? Will you need time and a place to exercise vigorously? How can your spouse or other family members help you with that?)

♦ Whom would you trust without question to care for your baby? (Yourself? Your spouse? Your mother? A nurse? A neighbor? A baby-sitter?)

♦ Whom would you not trust to care for your baby? (Yourself? Your spouse? A neighbor? A teenaged baby-sitter? How are you making these judgments?)

♦   ♦   ♦

BUILDING YOUR CHILD-CARE SUPPORT SYSTEM

A typical child-care support system will comprise five components: family, friends, baby-sitters, professionals, and technology. By combining those components with some skillful planning and a bit of luck, you can make your baby's life and your own a lot less stressful.

Remember, it's a good idea to get your baby used to being cared for by several people besides yourself. For the first few months, your baby may not appear even to notice who's taking care of her. (Some parents find this very distressing. Don't worry. Your baby really does know who you are and has a special relationship with you. She just doesn't have many ways of showing it that don't involve putting her in a psychology laboratory.) Having other adults who care for her regularly may make it easier on both of you if, when she's about nine months old, she starts showing "stranger wariness," what used to be called "stranger anxiety."

Also, keep in mind that most adults and adolescents are pretty good at caring for babies. If they weren't, our species wouldn't have survived this long. But many new parents feel exceedingly protective of their babies. You suddenly insist on certain things being done certain ways—even though you hated that type of compulsivity in your parents when you were growing up. Is your sister holding your baby at too much of an angle? Is your neighbor not heating up your baby's formula to precisely the right temperature?

Odds are your baby doesn't care about these things at all. Your overprotectiveness is a way of channeling your underlying anxieties about your competence as a parent. By focusing on what other people may be doing wrong, you can avoid worrying about your own possible (and equally meaningless) shortcomings.

But some parents, fearing that all their anxieties are unnecessary, can deny some real and potential child-care problems. I'm a firm believer in trusting your negative instincts about the people who you're considering caring for your child. Remember, it's a parent's prerogative to say "no" without offering an explanation.

If you have family members living nearby, count yourself both lucky and increasingly unusual. Grandparents, aunts, and uncles have always been called upon as standby babysitters. Because we share our own childhood histories with them, we tend to trust them more than other people and, in turn, expect them to trust us. The vast majority of the time they are marvelous caregivers.

Unfortunately, there are times when that's not the case, and it can lead to a great deal of tension within your family. Parents feel caught in a bind. They don't know how to tell a relative that they simply don't feel comfortable with him or her caring for their child.

♦　♦　♦

HAVE FAITH IN YOUR
GUT FEELINGS

Once, when I appeared on a national television talk show dealing with parenting problems, the host introduced me to three sisters, two of whom didn't trust the third to baby-sit for their children. Even so, they still let her care for the kids, worrying all the while they were left there.

The reasons for and validity of their concerns soon became apparent. They told me stories of how their toddlers were found wandering nearly a quarter mile from their sister's home. ("Oh, there's nothing to worry about," said the third sister. "All my neighbors know who they are.")

When asked about protecting her sisters' and her own children from danger, the third sister replied, "How will my two-year-old know not to run out into the street unless he tries?" and "No one can tell me what to do since, if my children get hurt, I'll pay the medical bills!"

The sisters were absolutely right not to trust this woman with their children! She presented a clear case of child endangerment if not abuse, and needed some psychiatric help for herself as well. Her perceptions of reality were distorted. She had no regard for the children's safety. She didn't understand the limits of children's abilities to reason and to protect themselves.

Yet despite her blatantly unsafe behavior, her sisters continued to go against their better judgment and let this woman care for their children because she was a member of their family. I've seen the same thing happen in families where the grandmother was an uncontrolled alcoholic or the uncle had a history of child abuse. The women on the television program were making excuses for their sister because she was a family member. They felt that anything bad she did reflected on them.[1]

---

[1] Dr. Paul Meehl, one of my professors in graduate school at the Univer-

That's why it's so important to discuss ahead of time with your spouse which family members you feel uncomfortable about when you think of them caring for your children. You and your spouse may share the same worries about certain individuals, but not feel comfortable being the first to raise the issue.

The same holds true for the second component of your support system: friends. Just because someone's a good neighbor, tennis partner, or coworker doesn't mean that you should automatically feel comfortable letting him or her care for your baby. Still, friends can be a major part of your support system, especially if they have children of their own who are roughly the same age.

◆   ◆   ◆

COOPERATIVE VENTURES

One of the most successful and, unfortunately, underutilized ways of helping both your child and yourself is to arrange with a friend or neighbor to take care of each other's children for a certain number of hours each month. This sort of baby-sitting cooperative can work very well with groups of three or four families, although it's often best not to have the children from more than two together at the same time.

This seems to work out best when there's some formality to the agreement, such as holding a monthly meeting to arrange for times when you'll care for each other's children. It's also a good idea to keep written records of how many hours of baby-sitting each family does each month, so that everyone contributes their fair share and no one feels exploited.

sity of Minnesota, referred to this as the Uncle John's Flapjacks Phenomenon. It goes something like this: If you run across a stranger who spends his days just making pancakes, you wonder if he's crazy. But dear old Uncle John, who would make thousands of pancakes and store them in the attic—well, he was just eccentric. After all, he's a relative!

You can also encourage friends who would usually buy you a small holiday, birthday, or other gift to consider giving you a certificate valid for several hours of their time as a baby-sitter. I assure you, it will be one of the best gifts you'll receive all year.

When I use the term "baby-sitter" to describe the third part of your support system, I'm talking about someone who works part-time in your home, as opposed to full-time professional child-care providers such as nannies, operators of family child-care centers, and the like. Most are too young to be parents themselves although, if they come from a large family, they may have considerable experience caring for younger brothers and sisters.

Of all the child-care providers, we tend to pay the least attention to baby-sitters. We often regard them as a stopgap solution to a problem (How can I go out on Thursday evening?) instead of as important people in the lives of our children. That also leads us to pay less attention than we should to how we treat them. But by showing them the respect they deserve for what is really a difficult and important job, you can avoid many of the problems other parents face when they need a baby-sitter in a hurry.

◆   ◆   ◆

THE CARE AND FEEDING OF
THE ELUSIVE BABY-SITTER

A few years ago one of my employees showed up late for work because her seventeen-month-old son's baby-sitter had cancelled at the last minute. (She usually brought her infant daughter to work with her.) It was the latest in a series of frustrations she was having finding someone to help her out for a dozen or so hours per week.

"I'm looking for the type of baby-sitter I was when I was in high school," she said plaintively. "It's a constant problem. The other parents in my neighborhood won't give me the names of their good baby-sitters. They don't want them to be stolen away," she continued.

Parents searching for baby-sitters often receive a crash course in microeconomics. If you're trying to hire someone to look after your children on a summer morning or a Friday evening, you'll soon discover that you've entered a seller's market.

But with teenage sitters, the critical variable may not be how much money you offer or even what your children are like. Baby-sitters often rate their employers more by the quality and abundance of the snacks they leave than by the behavior of their children. (Having a reputation for providing two pieces of cake, a pizza, or a pint of the latest gourmet ice cream can sometimes mean the difference between finding a sitter and not.)

Adults who baby-sit—not including those who provide full-time child care either in their home or in yours—are relatively rare. While older adolescents may have the maturity and reliability parents want, they often prefer to take jobs in fast-food restaurants since they see them as offering higher status. That's because, unlike baby-sitting, there's a minimum age for such workers. (Actually, teenagers and adults can sometimes make more money baby-sitting even though they may have a lower hourly wage, since they're almost always paid in cash and seldom report the income on their tax returns.)

That leaves the younger adolescents, who may not have the maturity and judgment you want in someone who cares for your child, even for a few hours. One response to the shortage of older, experienced baby-sitters has been the development of formal courses and videotapes that help early adolescents learn the rudiments of child care.

Baby-sitting courses are now offered by the Red Cross, YMCAs, churches and synagogues, and scouting groups. In addition to learning how to change a diaper and play with a toddler, such training often emphasizes what to do in a crisis, such as a fire or a medical emergency. The courses include basic first aid and CPR, as well as elementary work etiquette. ("Never eat the first or the last piece of anything in the refrigerator" is a common guideline.) There are also some programs on videotape that help young teenagers and even experienced baby-sitters learn some of the tricks of the trade, review emergency procedures, and give them some insight into child development.

These courses and videotapes also provide teenagers with a much-needed sense of status for what they're doing. Young adolescents respond very well to the "professionalism" that goes along with a scouting merit badge or a diploma from completing a course in baby-sitting. The certificates are tangible signs that they are progressing toward some of the responsibilities and privileges of adulthood. For many children, baby-sitting is a way to test new ways of relating to adults as peers rather than superiors. Being aware of adolescents' needs to see signs of their development into young adults can make hiring and retaining baby-sitters easier for parents.

Here are some things you can do when you're looking for and working with a baby-sitter that can make things easier for everyone involved:

♦ Interview prospective sitters during the daytime, ideally a few days before you need them. Be clear about your expectations, such as when they will arrive and what they will do for your children. Talk about what they'll be paid and what types of food you'll leave for them to eat.

Remember the adolescent's need for social status. The more you treat them like employees instead of just children from the neighborhood, the more likely they'll rise to your expectations and standards, and follow your instructions.

♦ Ask specific questions about how she would handle an emergency, such as a child who bumped his head, a small fire in the kitchen, or a power outage. Also ask about safety issues, such as what she would do if she were bathing the child and the telephone rang. (She should simply let it ring.)

You might even ask her to role-play what she would

say if your child was injured or if someone knocked on the door. Remember that your having high but realistic standards for the job will often make it more attractive.

♦ Pay the baby-sitter to spend some time with your child while you are there. Let the child get used to the sitter, and let the sitter learn, for example, how you prepare your baby's bottle or the rituals you use to put her to bed.

♦ In addition to leaving written information on where you can be reached and information about the child's bedtime and feeding, it's a good idea to show the sitter where you keep such things as flashlights and first-aid supplies. You should also write down and show her such things as where the fuse box or circuit breakers are, where the shut-off valve for the water is, and other emergency measures.

♦ Have an emergency information sheet near the telephone that, in addition to emergency phone numbers and the name and number of a nearby friend or relative, lists your name and street address. During the stress of an emergency, a baby-sitter may give the police, ambulance, or fire department her own home address instead of yours.

♦ Give the baby-sitter a spare set of keys to keep in her pocket. A pediatrician friend of mine who runs an emergency phone service says that they regularly receive phone calls from baby-sitters who have locked themselves out of the house, leaving the children inside.

♦   ♦   ♦

USING TECHNOLOGY TO YOUR ADVANTAGE

There are two other components to your child-care support system: professionals and technology. Locating and working with professional child-care providers are complex enough to warrant a chapter on their own—the next chapter, in fact.

Too few parents use technology to their advantage when they are arranging for child care. It may be because we tend to think of what our parents did when we were growing up. Usually, they just gave the baby-sitter the telephone number of the place where they were going, and perhaps called once or twice—as much to check up on the sitter as to see whether we were behaving.

The problem arises when you'll be in several places or in a place that doesn't have a telephone. Having a cellular phone can help. But even pocket-size cellular phones are, for the time being at least, expensive and relatively bulky. One solution is to carry an electronic digital pager, which in 1992 cost less than a dollar per day if you rented it by the month. It's small enough to clip to a belt or fit into a purse. If you'll be going to a concert or some other place where you wouldn't want the pager to beep, it can be set to vibrate silently instead.

The display on the pager will show a series of numbers that the caller enters on the keypad of the telephone they're using. (Usually, but not always, they'll simply enter the number they're calling from.) Although they're usually rented to businesses, pagers are a simple way for a baby-sitter or child-care provider to get in touch with you in an emergency.

What I do, in addition to leaving the baby-sitter with information about where I'll be, is leave a printed sheet posted on the refrigerator door with information on how to call the pager. I have the baby-sitter practice calling me while I'm standing right there, both to check that the pager is working, and to make sure she knows how to call it.

If it isn't an emergency—say, she wants to know if our son has to finish eating his vegetables—she dials the pager and enters our home telephone number. If it is an emergency, such as a broken faucet that has water shooting across the bathroom, she dials the pager and enters 999-9999. That way my wife and I know we have to respond immediately. What's important is that we know that if we don't get the signal with all 9s on it, we don't have to worry.

One way for you to prevent the problem of the baby-sitter locking herself out, or of you forgetting to take your key back, is to install a lock that can work with a combination as well as a key. There are several types of these, including some that allow you to temporarily set an easily remembered four-digit combination (2-4-6-8, for example) to allow the baby-sitter to get back in quickly. When the baby-sitter's gone, you can disable that combination on the lock.

With infants and toddlers, it's also a good idea to have a baby monitor—essentially a wireless intercom that allows the baby-sitter to hear if the child's in distress. This should only be used when your baby's asleep in his crib, of course. Make sure you get one that has more than one channel for transmitting and receiving. You may discover, as my wife and I did one evening, that the baby you hear crying actually lives down the street! If that happens, just change channels.

CHAPTER 14

Finding Child Care

One child-care provider had a gun cabinet in the living room. Another had the children playing in the street. At another, a four-year-old opened the door.
—A FRUSTRATED MOTHER I INTERVIEWED, WHO WAS SEARCHING FOR SOMEONE TO CARE FOR HER CHILD WHILE SHE WORKED

For many parents, getting occasional help from family, friends, and baby-sitters isn't enough. Anywhere from a few weeks to a few months after birth, they turn to child-care professionals ranging from live-at-home nannies to large commercial centers for help.

This is often a difficult decision, followed by an even more difficult search. If you're currently pregnant, the time to start looking for professional child care is *now!* If you wait until the last minute, you may find yourself hiring a person or contracting with a family child-care provider or commercial center that you're not comfortable with.

It's critically important that you do your homework, talk to other parents, visit some centers and family child-care homes, and check out the people you're thinking of hiring. Don't rely on licensure and training certificates—many of them are meaningless.

Caring for children is a huge business, yet much of it is

unregulated. It's not uncommon for local and state governments to have stricter standards for the people who cut your hair than for those who care for your children. Obtaining a child-care license may involve little more than filling out a form and paying a fee. One survey of child-care providers conducted by the American Academy of Pediatrics showed why it's so important for parents to thoroughly research where they send their children.

> Critical health and safety regulations in many states are inadequate, vague, or nonexistent. . . . One-quarter to one-half of states that license child care miss crucial health and safety standards needed to protect children such as: handwashing, pre-employment staff health evaluation, staff-infant ratio, and staff training. . . . Even in states with better regulations, lack of inspections and poor enforcement provide little assurance of quality in licensed child care programs.[1]

This information is even more distressing when you realize that the survey only looked at licensed providers, but most children are cared for in facilities that are not licensed and, therefore, never inspected. (Not being licensed isn't the same thing as illegal. The need for licensure often depends upon the location and the number of children being cared for.) This doesn't mean that unlicensed providers are necessarily worse than licensed ones. Many do an excellent job—they just choose to avoid the paperwork and other hassles involved.

CHOOSING AN IN-HOME
CHILD-CARE PROVIDER

Some parents decide that they want and can afford child care from someone who comes into their home, either to live or to work during the day. There are wide variations in the skills, competence, and knowledge of the people wanting to

---

[1] "National Survey Finds Wide Gaps in Child Care Health and Safety Standards," American Academy of Pediatrics, September 6, 1989.

be live-in nannies or other in-home child-care providers. Also, this type of help is not for everybody. Even if you have the extra room where a live-in nanny can stay, you have to ask yourself how you'd feel having a stranger under your roof all the time.

Will you worry about your appearance or how neat the house is? Are you concerned about your privacy? If you're hiring someone young, will you wind up as that person's surrogate mother as well? If you're hiring someone older than you, will you feel like she's your mother? How will you handle your employee's social life and visitors? Are you willing to handle the paperwork, insurance, and taxes involved in having an employee? What will you do if that person becomes ill and can't work for a week or more?

While you may envision hiring someone like Mary Poppins, the people you interview may remind you more of the Wicked Witch of the West or Elmer Fudd. There's good reason for this, even though it may have little to do with the people you're interviewing. Almost all parents—especially new parents—are very protective of their children. There's a natural rivalry between parents and the people who look after their children during the day. As parents, we want our children to feel close (but not too close) to the other adults in their lives. We worry that, if those attachments are too strong, they will replace us in our child's eyes. Fortunately, that worry is unnecessary.

I've seen vivid examples of this inherent conflict in the tremendous difficulty some parents have selecting someone to care for their baby. The job applicants who appear very good may be seen as posing a threat to the parents' relationship with their baby. Those applicants who don't seem warm, loving, and competent enough to threaten the relationship, don't look good enough to hire for the job.

Many of the parents who feel overwhelmed by the ambivalent feelings they have toward the child-care provider are really feeling guilty or angry about leaving their children and returning to work before they are emotionally ready. Unable to vent those feelings at a spouse or employer, they deflect them toward others, including coworkers and child-care providers.

◆   ◆   ◆

TIPS FOR FINDING AN IN-HOME CHILD-CARE PROVIDER

Although some people manage to find an in-home child-care provider through a friend's referral, odds are you're going to have to either advertise or use an agency. (A fourth alternative is to contact a so-called nanny school. Some of these are legitimate, while others are little more than scams set up to extract training fees from the workers before they charge placement fees from families. These latter "schools" provide aspiring child-care workers with a few months of superficial training and a worthless diploma.)

The agencies for child-care workers also vary in quality. Some specialize in young foreigners ("au pairs") willing to work in exchange for room, board, a meager salary, and a chance to attend school part-time. These au pairs work out very well for some families. But interviewing them ahead of time is often impossible. Also, since you're usually hiring a late adolescent, you may find yourself thrust into the role of surrogate parent to a homesick teenager. (Don't brush off that possibility and the responsibilities that go with it. A friend of mine told me that her British au pair recently came to her for advice. The young woman was pregnant and trying to decide what to do about her baby, wanted to drop out of school, and thought about leaving the country. This is not what my friend thought their employer/employee relationship would be like.)

Other agencies handle American citizens and residents. Agencies justify their fees (usually a proportion of the employee's first year's salary—check with the agency for details) by screening applicants, verifying their backgrounds, and referring only the most appropriate and trustworthy ones. But that screening can range from thorough to nonexistent. Working effectively with an agency takes more than a simple phone call. The more details about the job, your home, and your expectations of the caregiver that you furnish, the better the agency can do its work.

Be prepared to provide very specific information about the skills, attitudes, and background of the person you're looking for, as well as details about the job. Where will the person sleep and eat? Are you expecting her to do things besides child care, such as cleaning or cooking? What are your expectations for overtime, evening, and weekend work? Will you require a probationary period?

Keep in mind that this person's primary responsibility is to your children. Asking a child-care provider to clean or cook may detract from the care your baby gets.

You should ask yourself these same questions if you're going to advertise the position yourself. Write up a job description, just as if the position were being offered by a corporation. Be specific (but realistic) in describing the skills and experience you're expecting, as well as the hours and the details of the work.

You might want to consider hiring someone who has a baby about the same age as your child. My wife and I tried this when we worked out of offices in our home in suburban Minneapolis. Both our child-care provider and our office manager became pregnant. A few weeks after giving birth, each of them started bringing their babies to work with them. Everyone benefited. The office manager got on-site child care from someone she trusted— a very valuable perk. The child-care provider got to keep working while caring for her new daughter. And our son got two new playmates. However, because there were now several children involved, it took more flexibility on everyone's part to handle scheduling problems due to illnesses, doctors' appointments, and vacations.

You might consider offering this as a part-time benefit as well. Our current in-home child-care provider in Cambridge, Massachusetts, has a daughter in kindergarten. She often brings her daughter to work with her during school vacations to play with our two-year-old son. Everyone benefits, especially the children.

One inexpensive but successful way of recruiting someone is to post the job description at local community colleges and trade schools, where you may find someone who needs to take a year or two off to earn some money. You can also take out an ad in the newspaper. It's often more efficient to advertise in weekly community papers or ethnic (i.e., Irish, Jewish, Cuban, Chinese) newspapers, instead of the big-city dailies. Their classified ads are very inexpensive.

Your ad should give details about the job and your family. I've found it useful to include constraints on when people can telephone you ("Call evenings between 6–8 P.M.") since, if the applicant won't follow that simple instruction, she probably won't follow more important ones in caring for your child.

Whether you're doing the advertising yourself or working with an agency, use brief telephone conversations with the applicants to select those people you'll interview in person. You should plan on interviewing a half-dozen people at the very least. You'll find a surprisingly large number—my experience is it's as high as one in four—don't show up for the interview, which also tells you how reliable they would have been as employees.

◆   ◆   ◆

SCREENING IN-HOME CHILD-CARE APPLICANTS

Narrowing down the job applicants can be a daunting task, even for someone experienced at interviewing job applicants at work. Some interesting dynamics come into play during the interviews. Does the applicant remind you of your mother? Is this a good thing or would it make you hesitate to express your desires? Are you tempted to hire someone because you sense they need nurturing themselves? (Don't do it.)

More so than in most jobs, when you're hiring a childcare provider you're looking for someone who's not only competent and reliable, but whose personality is compatible with yours. In a sense, you're hiring a temporary family member.

I recommend not talking to more than two or three job applicants a day, and dividing each interview into several brief stages. That way, if someone doesn't appear suitable, you don't have to waste your time with the next stage.

Take notes during the interview, since individuals' strengths and weaknesses will start to blur after the fourth or fifth person you talk to. Don't hire anyone on the spot, especially toward the beginning of your search, since the other applicants may be an even better match. Let the applicants know when you will be calling them to give them your decision.

Finally, don't feel you have to hire the best person from the group you've interviewed if you're still uncomfortable with that person. The job's too important. If you're sure your standards are realistic and appropriate, just start your search again. Consider raising the salary or making other adjustments that would make the job more attractive to the sort of person you'd like to hire.

◆   ◆   ◆

TIPS FOR INTERVIEWING PROSPECTIVE IN-HOME CHILD-CARE PROVIDERS

Give each interviewee a copy of your written job description, and go over it with them. When you ask them why they're interested in the job, you'll often get vague answers like, "Oh, I just *love* children!" Gently try to go beyond an answer like that so you can see how heartfelt it is. What do they love about children? If the response is equally vague ("I enjoy spending time with them" or "I love everything about them") the applicant may simply be telling you what she thinks you want to hear, but doesn't really believe herself.

Look for someone who can give you specifics like, "I enjoy watching how they learn new and more difficult things." A person who's thought about those details probably means what she says. Again, follow up by asking for specifics. Ask her to describe another baby she worked with who was learning to walk or to talk. Do her descriptions sound mechanical or excited? You want someone who can share the excitement of your baby's development with you.

Ask the applicants specific questions about emergencies. What would they do if the baby had a bad cut on his head? What if it wouldn't stop bleeding? What if your baby was choking? What if your baby stopped breathing? In addition to basic first-aid knowledge, look for someone who has a calm, reasoned approach, takes care of the baby first (she should put a pressure bandage on the wound before calling 911, if that's needed), and is willing to seek professional help quickly.

If the applicant says she's had a cardiopulmonary resuscitation (CPR) course, find out how long ago she took it and whether it included training and practice on infant emergencies as well as adult problems. It's always a good idea to send (and pay for out of your own pocket) anyone caring for your children to a CPR course. *That includes you, too.*

Ask her what she'd do if he was crying and wouldn't stop. What if he threw his bottle or food on the floor? (Both of these are normal behaviors, of course. If she talks about punishing the child, don't hire her.) Ask her when she would spank or slap an infant for something he did. *Anyone who would hit an infant for any reason shouldn't be working with children.*

If you think this job applicant is a good candidate, introduce her to your baby. Watch how she approaches him. Does she reach out and pluck him from his crib, or does she speak to him gently before touching him? That may give you some insight as to whether she's able to empathize with his feelings. Listen to what she says. Ideally (and unconsciously) she should talk quietly about things she sees ("Oh, you have such a cute nose and two beautiful brown eyes.") or he sees ("You seem to like my earrings, don't you?"). You don't want someone who sits there passively or carries your child like a sack of potatoes.

Ask the applicant to change your baby's diaper. Again, does she talk to your child while she does it, or does she do it mechanically? Does she wash her hands when she's done? (The failure of caregivers to wash their hands after changing a diaper is one of the main ways diarrheal diseases and other illnesses get spread so quickly in large child-care centers.)

◆   ◆   ◆

Get at least two references from the applicant. Ideally, these will be from previous employers. (Enthusiastic references from relatives and neighbors are worthless.) Call the references and, in addition to asking their general opinion of the applicant, find out what her previous job responsibilities were. Ask about her strengths and weaknesses. How often was she late? How did she respond when the previous employer's child was sick?

It's a good idea to be circumspect about the answers you receive from references, since former employers may be afraid of a lawsuit if they say anything negative about the applicant. You can get the gist of the relationship, however, if you ask the former employer if they would rehire the applicant for the same job. If the response is anything other than "Yes, immediately!" you should take a closer look at the applicant's job history and performance.

Finally, ask yourself some questions about the interview. How comfortable does she seem with a baby your child's age? How comfortable do you feel with the idea of leaving him in her care? You can expect to feel a little anxious. But if a little voice inside your head is telling you that something's wrong, listen to that voice.

FINDING A CHILD-CARE HOME OR CENTER

So-called family child care—almost always women who care for up to a half dozen or so children in their homes during the day—has both advantages and disadvantages compared with larger child-care centers, which are generally operated in a more rigid, businesslike way, and are sometimes centrally owned or franchised like fast-food restaurants.

Family child care tends to be less expensive, and provides a more intimate, homelike atmosphere. That lack of formality can be great—until the owner decides to move or go into a new business or even take a vacation for a couple of weeks. If there aren't other adults who know your child and who are poised to take over, you may be suddenly left without child care. The same things can happen if the caregiver becomes ill. Whenever you talk to someone offering family child care, find out about the systems she has in place for dealing with these issues.

Child-care centers have more employees (and often much higher employee turnover), so they can usually care for your child for more hours of the day and throughout the year, without interruptions for vacations and personal emergencies.

Since we tend to associate child care with home, most parents look for providers who are close to where they live. But it's often a better idea to look for a child-care provider who's closer to where you work. There are quite a few advantages—and only a few disadvantages—to this. You'll get to spend more time with your child. A child-care provider near work often costs less, since your child is spending fewer hours there—she's with you during your commute. Finally, you'll have more peace of mind knowing that, in the unlikely event something goes wrong, you'll be able to get there quickly.

But this approach doesn't make sense if your daily commute involves two hours on the New York City subway or its ilk. It can also be a problem if you have to travel out of town and your spouse works far away from your job, or if you're ill and want your child to be cared for during the day.

A growing number of far-sighted corporations are establishing or contracting for on-site child care for their employees. This makes a tremendous amount of sense, since it allows employees to concentrate on their work while they're at the job. They can also spend lunch hours with their children. If your employer offers such an arrangement, pay close attention to the number of infants they'll accept; there's usually a strict limit. State and local governments usually mandate a significantly lower child-to-caregiver ratio for infants than for toddlers.

◆   ◆   ◆

HOW TO EVALUATE A
CHILD-CARE CENTER

I'm going to tell you something that most expensive child-care centers will deny: *There is absolutely no relationship between the amount of money a child-care center charges and the quality of care your baby will receive.* A more expensive center may have newer toys and a nicer building, but that's relatively unimportant to your baby. The best child-care centers invest in hiring and retaining the best people, not buying the most toys.

The essence of good child care lies in the relationship between the children and the adults. A warm, loving relationship between child and caregiver, and openness and respect between caregiver and parents, are infinitely more important than the center's budget for equipment.

Child-care centers almost always reflect the personalities and interests of their directors. That's why you should insist on meeting with the director of each child-care center you're considering. Here are some other things to look for:

♦ Ask when you can drop by to visit the center. A good center will welcome you at any time. Don't even consider a child-care center that won't allow you to drop by to inspect it unannounced. Keep in mind, however, that the period immediately after lunch will give you the least information about how the center operates because most of the children will be napping or playing quietly.

♦ Ideally, you should visit a center you're considering at least twice: once in the morning when the children are being dropped off, and again in the afternoon when the parents are picking the children up. Even though your child may still be an infant, pay attention to the facilities for and treatment of the older children. (Yours will be there soon enough.)

How do the children handle the separation from their parents? How do the child-care providers help with that separation? Does the child know what to do as soon as she enters? Does the child-care provider tell all the children what they should do all the time? (Not a good idea.) Do the children always choose what they will do? (Also, not a good idea. Ideally, there should be a combination of structure and freedom, with the children making many of the choices within constraints set by the adults.)

♦ Although its structure may be different, the child-care center should have the same functional areas as a house. There should be an area that acts like a living room or family room, where the adults and children will spend much of their time playing and reading. There should be comfortable places to sit, and accessible (and inaccessible) storage areas for toys and personal belongings. This will probably occupy the bulk of the center.

There should be a "kitchen" area—not a real kitchen, but a place where children can get dirty without the staff worrying about it. Usually this is a place where the children eat lunch and snacks, work with clay, paint, and do other "messy" jobs.

There should be an area that functions as a bedroom—
a quiet place where the children take naps. It's also
useful if there's a more isolated and smaller area for a
child who feels ill or extremely upset.

There should also be a bathroom. This should be
scaled down to the preschoolers' and toddlers' size so
that they can reach all the controls and don't have to
balance precariously on stepstools or boxes.

♦ Look at safety procedures and precautions. As I
mentioned earlier, it's often a good idea to get down on
your hands and knees to do some of this so that you can
see things from a child's perspective. Sharp edges and
corners of tables should be padded. Electrical outlets
should be capped. The phone numbers of the local poi-
son control center, police and fire departments, ambulance, et cetera. should be posted by the telephones in the
rooms where the children are, not just in the office.

Fire exits shouldn't be blocked. Doors to areas where
the children shouldn't go must be secured. Ask to see
the first-aid kit to find out how well it's stocked. Ask
how often they conduct fire drills. There should be no
smoking allowed on the premises. If you see anyone—
including a visiting parent—smoking anywhere near the
children, you should find another center.

♦ The infants' area should be self-contained and separate from the other parts of the "house." The first thing
you should do when you inspect this area is to smell it.
If the room smells more than a little bit of either human
waste or disinfectant, there may be an underlying public
health problem.

Watch how the caregivers change the infants' diapers.
Are there mirrors or other attractive things for the babies
to look at while they're on the changing table? Do the
caregivers speak to the babies while changing them, or
do they treat it as a purely mechanical chore? You want
a center where the caregivers use diaper changes as a
time for talking to the infants about what they look like
or what they're doing. An adult who simply wants to get
it over with as quickly as possible will be shortchanging
your baby in other areas as well.

Look at their procedures for preventing the spread of disease. Diarrhea is a major problem among children who attend child-care centers, as are respiratory illnesses. The rapid spread of such diseases can usually be traced to poor health-care procedures and lack of sanitary equipment. Is there a sink or two in the infants' room? Is there a soap dispenser and a sign reminding employees about proper sanitation? Are there sealed containers for soiled diapers?

Each child-care provider should do two things after every diaper change: She should immediately wash her hands with soap, and she should replace or disinfect the changing surface. If the center is using disposable paper covers on the changing tables, they should be thrown out and replaced after each diaper change. If they're not using paper covers, the surface should immediately be cleaned with a disinfectant, usually a diluted bleach solution. Also, see how they handle children who have runny noses. They should be sure to wash their hands with soap before touching another child.

Ideally, there should be one caregiver for every two or three infants. That's one of the reasons why infant care is so expensive. Watch how the caregivers handle babies who are upset. Are they patient? Do they talk soothingly? How do they act when they feed the babies? Do they allow them to interact with one another, or do they keep them isolated all day?

♦ Get references. Although many parents ask the center director to give them the names and telephone numbers of two or three parents, I don't think that's a good idea. The director will obviously give you the names of those families whom she feels are most satisfied.

Instead, ask for the names and telephone numbers of *all* the parents who have infants in the center. Ideally, you should call each of those parents—very few of even the largest centers care for more than a dozen infants at a time—to ask how satisfied they are. In any event, talk to more than two or three. It's well worth the added investment of your time.

Find out what they're most and least pleased about. Is

the center living up to its promises? Have other parents removed their children from the center recently? (If so, what are their names and phone numbers? If there have been more than one or two from your child's age group, you want to find out why.)

Don't expect every parent to be thrilled by everything the center is doing. Remember that there's a natural rivalry between parents and child-care providers. What you're looking for is patterns of comments that reveal the strengths and weaknesses of that particular center.

◆   ◆   ◆

CHAPTER 15

Cracking the Code
of Language

When I was born, I was so surprised I didn't talk for a year and
a half.

—GRACIE ALLEN

It may seem a little odd to include a chapter on language in
a book on pregnancy and infancy. After all, the word *infant*
comes from the Latin root meaning "not yet speaking." But
children are exposed to language from the moment they are
born and perhaps, according to some of the research I mentioned earlier, even while they're in the womb.

We bathe our children in words far more often than we
bathe them in water. It is an integral part of the parent-child
relationship. That's why I'd like to take a look not only at
how babies develop language, but how we use it as parents
in our efforts to communicate with them. Sometimes, the
words we say to our children tell us more about their development than the words they say to us.

Let's face it—all parents lie a bit when describing their
children's verbal accomplishments. There's nothing malicious about it. Our distortions, which are often unconscious,
are usually a cross between wishful thinking and foggy memories. ("Of course he's speaking early!" says a proud grand-

mother. "I remember when you were saying full sentences at ten months of age.") These revisionist family histories also show us how much attention we pay to our babies' attempts at speech, and how emotionally invested we all are in our children's use of language.

The ability to use descriptive spoken words separates us from other animals.[1] Our children seem more human and, as some parents describe it, more real once they start using language. We take particular pride if our children reach certain linguistic milestones ahead of other children of the same age. It's so important, that we unconsciously distort our perceptions of our babies' first utterances so that they register in our brains as words.

A baby who, while randomly exercising and exploring her ability to create sounds, says *muh* to her mother, will often be quickly rewarded with great attention and affection. "She knows who I am!" her mother would probably say. Her father, overhearing the same *muh* may interpret it quite differently but with equal conviction. "Listen to this! She's asking for some milk," he might cry out.[2]

These distortions of our perceptions play a critical part in our children's learning to speak. I'll describe how that works in greater detail later in this chapter. But for the moment, let's look at what parents do to encourage these verbal interactions.

[1]What's unique is the use of spoken words, not the ability to communicate. One of the most fascinating examples of other communication strategies discovered by ethologists is the honeybee's use of what's called a "waggle dance" to inform other members of the hive how far and in what direction relative to the sun (complete with a correction for wind drift) a field of flowers lies. Ever since memorizing the details of waggle dance interpretation for an examination in graduate school, I've wondered when that particular set of facts would come in handy. It finally has. Thank you. I feel much better now.

[2]It's also important to remember that a child who says "dada" before saying "mama" is not expressing a preference for a particular parent or otherwise passing judgment. It's largely a reflection of which sound is easier for your child to make.

Children's first step toward speech is triggered by the adults in their household. It's always impressed me how often and with such great enthusiasm parents—especially mothers—talk to newborn babies who are incapable of answering back. These aren't just parents who've read books on the importance of a child's early exposure to language. We see this in diverse families from cultures all over the world, and have no reason to doubt that it's been going on for countless generations.

I once mentioned to another psychologist my observation about how persistently adults talk to a baby who cannot respond in kind. He said I shouldn't be surprised, and pointed out some obvious things I had failed to notice. After all, he continued, people (including me) talk to their pets, their plants, and occasionally their television sets. When we're lonely, need reassurance, or want extra encouragement, we'll even sometimes talk to ourselves out loud.

Dr. Naomi S. Baron, a professor of linguistics at the American University in Washington, D.C., refers to this behavior as "the conversational imperative."[3] We all feel a pressure to speak when we're in a social situation. You can see a good example of this on many European trains, where the passengers sharing a compartment may have no languages in common. Yet most of the time they will try to talk to each other, switching from native tongues to gestures to drawings in an attempt to get their information across. To be more easily understood, they will simplify their grammar, repeat critical phrases, and look intently for a sign that their words have bridged the gap.

This is similar to how adults talk to babies. But there are additional aspects of parent-infant communication that we often do unconsciously. If you understand what typically makes up this special type of interaction, you'll see why some of it is so useful and other parts, quite frankly, are mysterious and perhaps worthless.

[3]N. S. Baron, *Growing Up with Language: How Children Learn to Talk* (Reading, MA: Addison-Wesley, 1992).

BABY TALK

You've probably noticed how adults often talk differently to babies than to other adults or even toddlers. They raise the pitch of their voices and do other things we would consider inappropriate or insulting in normal adult conversation. A few even have their voices take on a saccharine quality guaranteed to nauseate any nonparent (and even some parents) in the room.

We generally refer to this shift in tone, syntax, and attitude as "baby talk." It's something that we expect in that particular interaction, so much so that an adult who approaches a newborn with serious demeanor and says, "It's good to see you again, Robert. How was your day?" would be regarded as insensitive to children, or worse. Yet those words have no less meaning to the baby than a more socially acceptable statement like, "Oh, what a cute little tummy you have!"

I remember one time when my son, then eighteen months old and sitting in his stroller, and I were going to get some food from a local market. My son was very sociable and outgoing. He'd learned quickly that if he said "Hi!" to an adult he was likely to get a response and some extra attention. As we walked to the store he would cry out a greeting to every passerby, each of whom answered him and made a comment like, "Oh, aren't you cute." Needless to say, he basked in the limelight of this extra attention.

As we approached the market he spied a woman in a business suit coming toward us. "Hi!" he cried. But she had her nose buried in a report of some sort while she walked. "Hi!" he yelled once more, only louder. Again she gave no response. Finally, he waited until she was only two feet ahead of his stroller and bellowed "HI!!!"

The woman stopped dead in her tracks, looked at him with surprise and muttered, "Oh, um, hello. I mean, good evening. Sorry, but I have to go." It was hysterically funny, not because anything she said was outlandish or inappropriate, especially if she had been talking to another adult. What made it funny, and what probably made her stumble over her words as well, was that she was unable to mentally switch gears to how she was expected to talk to a young child.

What's going on when we engage in baby talk is more than "cute" or "simple" speech. There's a clear but complex pattern that includes not only a higher-than-normal pitch, but a greater range of tones which reinforce the emotional content of the message. We also drag out certain words for emphasis, such as "Oh, you're such a *g-o-o-d* girl! You finished your *w-h-o-l-e* bottle." We also tend to speak more slowly, with simpler grammar and with clearer enunciation, much as we might when talking to an adult who wasn't fluent in our language.

Parents of babies and even toddlers often verbalize both sides of their conversation, either implicitly or explicitly. "Would you like some mashed banana? Oh, you would. Well, I'll get you some." We may be inordinately descriptive, assigning names to objects, emotions, and status, often doing so with a good deal of repetition. "That's your teddy bear, Chrissie. He's a big teddy bear, a brown teddy bear." "My, you sound cranky today! Didn't you get enough sleep?" or "Let me put on your diaper. First this side. Then the other side. Now, it's *a-l-l* done."

There appear to be clear reasons for and benefits from these utterances. A higher-pitched voice seems more attractive to babies. Slowing down the speed, simplifying grammar and syntax, naming objects and emotions, describing status, and modeling conversations all make it easier for a child to puzzle through what language is all about.

Similarly, using a child's name instead of a pronoun ("That's Debbie's rattle" instead of "That's your rattle") probably helps a child understand her name. But one of the most surprising aspects of baby talk is the way we use diminutives and other special words with babies that we don't use with adults. For example, when my son was very young I found myself saying "doggie" and "puppy" to him instead of "dog," and referring to our two cats as "kitties." If anything, doggie, puppy, and kitty are more complex words than dog and cat. (Several times I caught myself referring to one of our cats, who is named Zabar, after one of my favorite stores in Manhattan, as "Zabar-kitty"—which is both conceptually and phonetically much more complex than necessary.)

I've heard many parents do the same thing, substituting "tummy" for "stomach" or saying "choo-choo train" instead of simply "train," for example. We'd never expect an adult to complain of a tummyache or a commuter to talk about taking the 8:05 choo-choo train. Why do we use words like that with children? By using more complex words, it's almost as if we wanted to make language more difficult for them to acquire.

One compelling theory is that we talk to babies this way not so much for their sake, but for ours. By shifting our patterns of speech we are acknowledging our special relationship with babies. The real purpose (and benefit) of baby talk is to bolster the social interaction between parent and child. Shifting our style of speech forces us to pay more attention to what we say and, therefore, to the person we're talking to. The topic and details of the conversation don't matter much. It's the emotions and the extra attention that convey the most important message—to both generations.

EARLY SPEECH

Although most parents tend to view their children's linguistic growth as separate from their physical maturation, the two are woven together, especially during infancy and early toddlerhood. For example, a child may start rhythmically repeating the same sound (ba-ba-ba-ba) soon after she starts using her fine-motor coordination to make rhythmic motions over and over with her hands and fingers. That's why it's a good idea to look at the two together, so that you can see how they're coordinated.

Child development books are filled with charts that tell you how many words your child should know, and how complex her sentences should be at various ages. As with all such developmental charts, they are rough approximations at best. The difference between being at the 35th percentile and the 95th percentile in vocabulary at twelve months of age is much less important than the child's overall physical and mental development. But if a child seems to be taking no interest in understanding words, or isn't responding to sounds the way other children her age do, she should be checked by her pediatrician.

You should also pay attention if your child frequently plays with or tugs at her ears. This may be a sign of a middle-ear infection (*otitis media*), which can usually be treated easily with medications. (Remember that although the symptoms of a middle-ear infection caused by bacteria and treated with antibiotics will usually get better within a day or two after starting treatment, you should keep giving your baby the medication for the total number of days your pediatrician prescribes. Otherwise the infection may come back immediately, and with worse symptoms. It's also a good idea to talk to your pediatrician about the possible side effects of the medication, since switching types of antibiotics can often help.)

If there are repeated episodes of middle-ear infection, your pediatrician may talk to you about having your baby undergo a minor surgical procedure to install tiny plastic tubes in her eardrum to allow drainage and equalize the pressure. I mention this problem because chronic ear infections are sometimes associated with delays in language development, especially if those infections are not treated.

♦ ♦ ♦

THE LANGUAGE GAME

Children learn language largely through copying the people around them. That's why it's so important to talk to and read to your baby from the day she's born. (More on that in the next few pages.) There also seems to be a biological pressure or drive to make noise, which is why deaf infants will also babble.

The odds are that your child's first vocal expression was a cry, delivered with great indignation upon his entry into the world. At that point, his ability to make sounds was limited to a few soft snorts, grunts, and that omnipresent and highly effective wail. As his vocal tract matures over the next month or two, he'll start making cute little cooing noises.

These sounds come at a critical time in your relationship with your baby, for the odds are you're frustrated, sleep-deprived, and emotionally overwhelmed. Those cute little coos catch your attention. You respond to them by talking back quietly but enthusiastically to your baby. "Well, hi there! You seem to be happy this morning."

Your baby knows a good thing when he hears it. It may take him a few times before he sees the connection, but eventually he recognizes that you'll pay extra attention to him in a very nice way when he makes certain sounds. So he keeps cooing and trying other sounds to see how you will respond.

I think of this as the first stage of the language game that all children play as they're trying to make sense of the words they hear and the sounds they can make. Within a few months, your baby will be able to babble a wider range of sounds, some of which will capture your attention more consistently than others. They'll shift from single sounds (fff, buh) to repeated sounds (mama, gaga). Soon, they'll make these sounds with the rhythm and inflection that reflect the syntax of the language they've been hearing. This "jargoning," as it is sometimes called, sounds like English, French, Chinese, or whatever language is spoken at home, but it is made up of nonsense syllables.

Soon after that, your baby will begin associating words or sound patterns with objects. Many parents instinctively promote that important transition by naming objects when they talk to their babies much more than they would with older children. "Those are your *toes*. And controlled sounds can convey information. This is a more complex concept than many of us realize, since it seems so obvious to adults.

Yet many parents miss much of the beauty of that important discovery. Although we tend to pay attention to the words our children say, we can marvel at their development even more by thinking of language as music rather than clusters of letters. So often we pay attention to the lyrics, and ignore the rhythms and melodies our children are composing as they learn to talk. But language is not spoken in a lockstep monotone. So much of the meanings of words, in English especially, is conveyed by pauses, emphasis, and inflection.

When we talk to babies, we speak in italics and capitals, and fill our short phrases with dramatic punctuation. We raise the pitch of our voices more than usual at the end of a sentence when we ask a baby a question, even though we don't really expect to hear an answer. "Are you hungry? I thought so." "Oh, what CUTE little FINGERS you have! Let's count them. One . . . two . . . three . . . four . . . F-I-I-IVE!"

The shifting tone means far more to us than to our newborn children. In fact, when children begin to speak, it's common for them to make one-word statements that sound, because of their rising inflections, like they are questions. The young toddler who sounds like he's saying "Hungry?" is probably thinking "I'm hungry now!" rather than asking whether you wish to join him for breakfast.

The pauses and emphasis of certain words convey to the child the complex syntax of the language. We can hear this sense of pacing imposed on our children's experimentations with sound as they grow older. Their babbles and first words become more complex, but not randomly so. Children play with the melodies and rhythms of speech as much as they play with the words themselves.

That's why, as I said earlier, it makes so much sense to read aloud to your baby from the very beginning. Although we tend to read to older children to convey the content of a story, babies and young toddlers respond to different aspects of that pleasant interaction. They are enraptured by the music you have ten of them. Ten *toes!*" This helps babies crack the code of spoken language. But it's important to remember that you're not preparing your child for a quiz. Don't expect, even when your baby has started to use words, that he'll remember a particular one if you use it ten or fifteen or twenty times during the day.

Each baby has to crack the language code at his own pace. While some adults and older children who have excellent verbal skills were early talkers, others took a lot longer before using words, but made up for lost time over the next few months. If you have fun talking to your baby, he'll enjoy listening to the music of your voice. If you push too hard to "teach" him to speak, you'll both become frustrated, and you'll miss the enjoyment of watching your baby discover language.

This doesn't mean that you should just prattle on mindlessly, filling a room with words so that your baby will hear them. Remember that you're having conversations with your child. Ask him questions and pause for a response, even though you know he will not answer.

Also keep in mind that in the beginning, your baby won't necessarily understand the meaning of the word the same way you do. For quite a few months, my son apparently knew that "mommy" referred to his mother, but he referred to any adult man as "daddy" and any older woman as "grandma." (Actually, he called the cats "daddy" for a while too—probably just to annoy me and keep me in my place.)

◆　　◆　　◆

THE MUSIC OF LANGUAGE

The steps toward mastering the first few words are at least as impressive as children's tremendous spurt in language acquisition that comes a year or so later. In those early months, the child is struggling with the idea that voluntary, of your voice. Your focused attention is soothing and reassuring. The messages you convey are very powerful, even before the words themselves have meaning.

That's probably why babies seem to love listening to poetry, even though it makes as much sense to them as a stock market report. We naturally read poetry differently from prose, for we pay closer attention to its rhythms and enjoy its rhymes. It doesn't have to be "children's" poetry either. Rather, it should be something that you particularly enjoy as a parent, so that you can convey that sense of pleasure and excitement.

The same holds true for singing, and why babies pay close attention when we sing to them, even if our voices are off-key. There's something special about the way we treat words in a song. Your baby will hear the patterns of the words and, as you repeat it over time, will anticipate the sounds with great relish.

Again, keep in mind that you're not "teaching" your child to speak the same way that you may have been taught algebra or history at school. Your baby is already primed and motivated to learn, if you'll simply allow him. And with your help, he'll slowly decipher the mysterious code of language and, through that act, become more human   and more fun.

CHAPTER 16

The Journey to Toddlerhood

Crawling is not a necessary developmental milestone. Some of
the smartest children I know displayed the most bizarre meth-
ods of locomotion before walking. Some roll over and over, and
one little girl sat in a half-lotus position and scooted backward
wherever she wanted to go.
                                          —LORAINE STERN, M.D.[1]

Pregnancy and infancy take you and your child on a journey
filled with surprises, even for the most experienced parent or
child development expert. That's part of the beauty of this
time of life. There are so many variations on the themes of
childhood, each creating its own melody and harmonies with
the music of the parents. Each dissonant chord eventually
gets resolved as both of you change in response to each other.

    You and your child have undergone profound changes
since his conception. I remember, as my own son was approaching toddlerhood, thinking that so many of the things
that had caught me emotionally off-guard as a new parent,
now seemed so normal. My wife shared similar and comple-
mentary feelings. We had trouble recalling a time when we

[1]L. Stern and K. Mackay, *Relax and Enjoy Your Baby* (New York: Norton,
1986), p. 204.

didn't have to change diapers every few hours. We noticed that we hadn't seen a movie or a play in a theater for months. Our social life was dramatically different.

Most important, both my wife and I had come to realize at a deep and profound level that we were *parents*. We had carried on the tradition of our ancestors, and hoped our son would do the same. We noticed that our friends and neighbors who had children treated us a little differently. It was as if we had joined a club whose initiation rites bonded us to its other members across cultures and across time.

Parent: It's a label that will stick with us for the rest of our lives, no matter what else we do or where we live or whom we know. *Parent*.

And I noticed that, as a parent, I'd started viewing all children a little differently. Strangers' babies looked much cuter—though not as cute as my own child, of course. I'd helped more than a few mothers on airplanes who were trying to comfort an upset child, instead of grumbling to myself about the annoyance. I could no longer keep the same level of clinical detachment when I heard about child abuse or crib death. I became furious when I saw children standing on the front seat of a moving car instead of being strapped into a car seat.

In addition to becoming a parent to my child, I felt like a parent to all children. It was a surprisingly good feeling. I played more easily with children from the neighborhood, and had more fun doing it. I'd reorganized my work schedule to allow for more family time.

There were other, less profound reminders of how I had changed since my son's birth. On several occasions when he was about a year old, I found myself waking up with the words of a song rattling around in my head. That wasn't particularly unusual for me. It's just that these days the songs were from *Sesame Street*. You really know you're a parent when the first words you think of in the morning are "Sing what I sing. Sing after me" or, worse than that, "I'm an aardvark, and I'm proud! I'm an aardvark, and I'm happy!" (Those of you who cannot read those words without thinking of the melodies know exactly what I'm talking about.)

♦   ♦   ♦

A QUICK LOOK BACK

As your child's first birthday draws near, it's useful to take a few minutes to ponder some of the changes you and your family have undergone, and to compare notes with your spouse, parents, or siblings, or a close friend who's seen you through the past few years.

As with the earlier questionnaires, it's a good idea to write down your answers independently and to keep them short. Also remember that the possible answers I list are simply to trigger your thinking. You don't have to select any of them.

♦ The first thing that comes to mind when I think of my child is _____. (Pride? Work? Love? Disappointment? Excitement? A sense of accomplishment?)

♦ The thing about my child that took me the most by surprise is _____. (Her looks? Her dependence on me? Her rapid growth? Her slow growth? Her constant demands?)

♦ What surprised me the most about being a parent was _____. (The amount of effort it takes? The lack of sleep? The rewards? The frustrations? The effect on other areas of my life? The effect on my marriage?)

♦ My family and my spouse's family have been _____. (Supportive? Absent? A source of information and perspective? A source of pressure?)

♦ I wish my child were _____. (Older? Quieter? Still a baby? Less sensitive? More independent? Like my friends' children in certain ways? A boy/a girl?)

♦ When it comes to our child's daily care, my spouse is _____. (More involved than I predicted? Not involved enough? Very anxious? Too bossy?)

♦ Over the next year or so, I think my child will be-

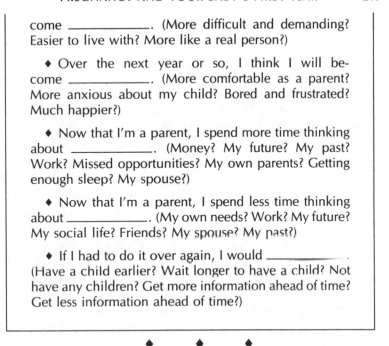

come _____. (More difficult and demanding? Easier to live with? More like a real person?)

♦ Over the next year or so, I think I will become _____. (More comfortable as a parent? More anxious about my child? Bored and frustrated? Much happier?)

♦ Now that I'm a parent, I spend more time thinking about _____. (Money? My future? My past? Work? Missed opportunities? My own parents? Getting enough sleep? My spouse?)

♦ Now that I'm a parent, I spend less time thinking about _____. (My own needs? Work? My future? My social life? Friends? My spouse? My past?)

♦ If I had to do it over again, I would _____. (Have a child earlier? Wait longer to have a child? Not have any children? Get more information ahead of time? Get less information ahead of time?)

♦   ♦   ♦

A NEW PERSPECTIVE

We each develop a new sense of perspective on life during our child's first year. We shift our values and perceptions in many small ways, some barely noticeable by themselves. Taken as a whole, however, these small changes signal a revolution in who we are and how we look at the world.

Part of that new sense of perspective that parents develop is distorted. It is a necessary and occasionally useful distortion, however. We pay close attention to things we never gave a second thought to in years past and, for the first few weeks at least, become sensitive to the slightest noise our children make in the dead of night.

I've talked to many parents who say they sleep much better when they have a cold than when their child does. It's a fascinating paradox, to suffer symptoms more greatly when someone else is ill. It speaks to the intensity of the relationship between parent and child.

We can see these distortions every day in pediatricians' offices and emergency rooms, where kids who have minor injuries or illnesses are brought in by parents who are far more upset than their children. When I worked as a blood technician at a pediatrics hospital years ago, I remember how common it was for parents to wince or even make a noise when I drew blood from their children. The emotional bonds within these families were so strong that the parents felt the fleeting pain of the needle or lancet with their children or, perhaps they hoped, instead of them.

But it is the worries that are the most striking—and usually the most distorted. We suddenly become aware of why our own parents paid such close attention to what we did, who we were with, and how we dressed. "I'm cold, so you should put on a sweater," doesn't seem as outlandish a statement anymore. We can almost hear ourselves saying it in a few years.

We find ourselves worrying more about what things will be like after we have died, for now there's a part of us who will be there to enjoy or suffer the consequences of what we leave behind. Sometimes it's the actions spurred on by those thoughts that allow us to give our children—all children— their greatest gifts.

◆   ◆   ◆

THINK HORSES, NOT ZEBRAS

I'd like to end the final chapter of this book on the same note on which I began the introduction: with a story about my own shortcomings as a parent. Like so many of these stories, it seems funny in retrospect. At the time, however, my emotions were dramatically different. It's also a good transition to the next book in this series, which deals with toddlerhood and the preschool years.

The phrase "Think horses, not zebras" will sound familiar to just about any American-trained physician or clinical psychologist, and perhaps to those who've studied those fields in other countries as well. It describes one of the fundamental rules of diagnosis.

The words refer to a common mistake medical students make when they have to diagnose patients: They don't take into account the relative likelihood of different problems that have some of the same symptoms. The full phrase is, "When you hear hoofbeats on the Western plains, think horses, not zebras."

Let me give you an example: You've come home from a picnic on a hot July day. While there, you ate some potato salad that had been sitting in the sun all afternoon. A few hours later, you develop a stomachache, diarrhea, and nausea. Any experienced physician or public health practitioner would immediately say that the most likely cause of your problem was food poisoning. (Certain bacteria enjoy potato salad even more than people do. That's why contaminated potato salad is one of the classic sources of food poisoning.)

But a new medical student who has little experience with patients, and who had recently boned up on digestive diseases for an examination, would proudly point out another possible diagnosis involving some obscure parasites that live in tropical rain forests and can cause those same symptoms.

She'd be right, of course. A rare parasite is a possibility. But it's thousands or millions of times more likely that your symptoms were caused by tainted potato salad, especially if you haven't been hiking through rain forests recently. It's the same as hearing those hoofbeats on the Western plains. Sure, they *could* be coming from a herd of zebras that escaped from the local zoo, but if you had to put money on it, you'd probably bet they came from horses, not zebras.

What does this have to do with being a parent? Well, sometimes we make those same mistakes with our children, either out of naïveté or because of our close emotional involvement with them. Just as it's tempting to look at sitting up or talking early as a sign of our children's superior intelligence, we also run the risk of misinterpreting small, temporary, and normal problems as potential disasters. Let me give you a personal example:

One afternoon, when my son was about twelve months old and had recently learned to walk, I noticed that he seemed to be having trouble with his coordination. His gait was more awkward. His balance was less steady than usual. His head tilted slightly to one side.

As a psychologist who has done many hundreds of brain-damage evaluations, I immediately started looking for signs of trouble. The more closely I studied him, the more I noticed subtle things that just weren't right. These were small behaviors to which I would never have paid attention had I not been thinking of all the things that might be going wrong.

As I grew increasingly worried, I started thinking about whom I would send him to for an evaluation. Since my son hadn't slept yet that afternoon, I put him to bed so that I could read up on the possible causes of his problem and become more familiar with the latest diagnostic procedures.

I kept wondering why I hadn't seen this problem before. Did he have a fast-growing tumor of some sort? Would he be permanently disabled or even die within a few months or weeks? How would I break the terrible news to my wife? The more I thought about it, the worse the diagnosis and prognosis seemed to be, and the more upset I became.

By the time my son woke up two hours later, I was approaching total panic. I gently lifted him from his crib to the ground to watch him walk. I wanted to see how quickly things were deteriorating, and braced myself for the worst.

Much to my surprise, his gait was perfect. So were his balance and coordination. Even his head wasn't tilted anymore. The cause of his problem, it seems, wasn't a rare tumor or obscure birth defect.

He'd simply needed a nap! And at that point, so did I.

♦   ♦   ♦

INDEX